Sonic to Sta

The Evolution of the British Nuclear Deterrent

*"Fear was always a bad counsellor,
and fear is no position from
which to view the world."*

Generaloberst Hans von Seeckt

V-Bomber Force

Flying in the Missile Age. The advent of the stand-off bomb (air-to-ground missile, for despatch several hundred miles from a target) greatly enhances the vital role of the V-Bomber Force for many years to come.

Aircrew Selection. First you go for 4 days to Hornchurch for a series of tests. Alertness of mind, as well as quickness of hand and eye, will stand you in good stead.

Basic Training. Once through Hornchurch, you are a potential officer, ready to do your basic training. This you finish with the rank of Acting Pilot Officer. Then begins your flying training during which you do your first solo flight.

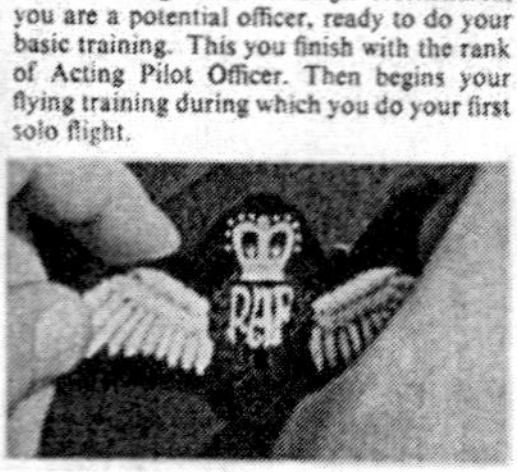

Passing Out. Advanced flying training takes you to aerobatics, formation flying and instrument flying. Once you successfully complete your course on Vampire jets, the great moment comes, at the passing out parade, when you step forward for your 'wings'

Joining a Squadron. First you go to an Operational Conversion Unit. Soon after you qualify you are shaking hands with your new squadron commander. Your life in a bomber squadron has begun.

To fly Britain's V-Bombers calls for a highly developed sense of responsibility, and the men who fly them must also have more than a fair share of skill and initiative. How does an R.A.F. flying career begin? What, briefly, are the stages before you join the V-Bomber Force?

The Royal Air Force *Flying ...and a career*

How to Join. You can join the R.A.F. through the Direct Commission scheme, which offers you the choice of a permanent career right up to pension age or a twelve-year engagement with the option of leaving after eight. (If you leave after twelve years you take back to civilian life a tax-free gratuity of £4,000.) Alternatively, there's a five-year Short Service Commission. Whichever you choose, the pay is good. The new increases in pay and allowances, effective from the 5th April, mean that a Flight Lieutenant of 25 can, with full allowances, earn more than £1,500 a year. If you are between 17½ and 26, if you have the General Certificate of Education, the Scottish Leaving Certificate, or their equivalent, then write, stating age and education, to the Air Ministry, Dept. (VR13), Adastral House, London, W.C.1. We will send you all you need to know.

Sonic to Stand Off

The Evolution of the British Nuclear Deterrent

By

Alan Morrison

Publisher/graphic restoration: A. MacKay Ltd   Editor: Iain C. MacKay

ISBN: 978-0-9573443-4-1

For Chery. B. Many thanks.

Printed and bound in Scotland by Glasgow Cross Press,
37 High Street, Glasgow, G1 1LX
http://www.glasgowcrosspress.com/books.aspx
0141 552 551

Flying in the missile age

THE NEED FOR PILOTS, navigators and air electronics officers is as urgent as ever . . . and the career prospects no less promising. Weapons change, tactics change, but the role of the Royal Air Force today remains the same.

'I should like to say a word about the future of the Royal Air Force . . . The introduction of new weapons will be a gradual process, extending over a good number of years, and even then there will still remain a very wide variety of roles for which manned aircraft will continue to be needed. I therefore hope that young men who have the ambition to be pilots, as well as those who are interested in new technical advances, will continue as before to look to the R.A.F. for a fine and useful career.'

MINISTER OF DEFENCE, APRIL 16TH 1957

More opportunities — not less. Manned aircraft will *always* be needed for those functions to which the human brain in the air is indispensable. And, whatever new instruments of air power are evolved, the R.A.F. will always need men of initiative who have been trained to master the problems of the air, in the air. These men can not only fulfil their ambition to fly for as long as they serve, but will have a full and satisfying career.

A sure future — good pay. You can join the R.A.F. through the Direct Commission Scheme, confident of a permanent career right up to pension age. Or you can choose a twelve-year engagement with the option of leaving after eight. If you leave after 12 years you take back to civilian life a tax-free gratuity of £4,000! Alternatively, there is a five-year Short Service Commission Scheme, and for University Graduates, a special four-year Short Service Commission. Whichever you choose, the pay is good. At the new rates, a Flight Lieutenant of 25 for instance, can draw, with full allowances, about £1,500 a year.

The advent of the stand-off bomb (air-to-ground missile, for despatch several hundred miles from a target) actually enhances the vital role of the Valiant and other V-bombers for many years to come.

The Royal Air Force

Flying . . . and a career

How to fly with the R.A.F. You must be between 17½ and 25 and absolutely fit. You must have General Certificate of Education or Scottish Leaving Certificate or their equivalents. You must be able to lead others, and you must have aptitude as well as enthusiasm for flying. If you feel you have all these qualities, write at once for details of the schemes of entry and an informative booklet, to the Air Ministry (V.R.5), Adastral House, London, W.C.1. Give date of birth and educational qualifications.

Contents

Publisher's Statement

"Sonic to Standoff" arose from an entry in an archive document, in a series of minute notebooks, entitled, "Missile Work." It was established, through deep research, that the only missile work being carried out in the United Kingdom, post-war, was on the Vickers Trans-Sonic Missile. Air-launched by a Mosquito aircraft off Land's End, this missile proved the concept of a standoff weapon. It was powered by an RAE version of the Walter rocket motor, used in the German Me163 and a series of German anti-aircraft missiles. It was also used in a supersonic reconnaissance aircraft, which had been captured by the Russians and possibly by the British and Americans in 1945. The United Kingdom adopted the idea and by 1960, had produced the stand-off nuclear weapon, Blue Steel. Carried by the V bomber force, this missile became the basis of British nuclear deterrence from around 1963 until the end of 1970.

There existed a surviving series of overhead projector skins, with images of the evolution of British Nuclear weapons up to 1970, which had been used as presentation material. When the initial manuscript was prepared it had been heavily expanded. Much of the early German research was investigated, from 1919 to 1946 and the use of captured German data. Due to a change of circumstances, the manuscript was put in abeyance and resurrected many years later. Parts of the manuscript had already been published. The script became, *"... An unofficial history based on official documents."*

Netherton *7th September 2015*

Preface and acknowledgement

During the Second World War, the Royal Air Force became the principal striking force against Germany. Aircrews, Commonwealth, Empire, Free French etc., flew day and night operations from 1939 to 1945, using a variety of methods, including map and compass and electronic aids to reach their targets. One very important target was the German rocket testing station at Peenemunde. There were also the

Thousand Bomber raids on such targets as Cologne, Hamburg and the Ruhr. Achieving esprit de corps, the force even sent a Mosquito to interrupt a speech by Hermann Goering in Berlin ("The Big City") and dropped a French national flag on the Arc de Triomphe in Paris. The culmination of this professionalism can be clearly seen in Operation Chastise – "The Dams Raid" of 1943. Post-war, this was a much reduced force but was ready to take on the mantle of British defence and nuclear deterrence.

During the Second World War, Britain had become one gigantic aircraft carrier, being virtually covered with airfields. The main user of these airfields was the United States Army Air Force (USAAF) and as with the Royal Air Force, the crews flew their missions with élan and dedication. Both air forces turned from heavy, strategic bombing to tactical bombing in Operation Overlord, the D-Day landings. By this time, a bond had grown between the Americans and the British, starting in China in the Nineteenth Century, The Great War and at Shanghai in 1926. This was termed, "The Special Relationship."

With wartime Britain on the verge of collapse, Churchill sent a team to America to charm President Roosevelt for support. The team took with them details of all the secret work that was being undertaken by the wartime British. On viewing the documents, especially the Maud report on the Atomic Bomb, the Americans were intrigued and adopted much of what was on offer.

Britain's main post-war bomber was the Avro Lincoln, a development of the Lancaster. It could not carry a nuclear weapon, but some had been modified to carry the giant Tallboy series of bombs, including Grand Slam. There existed a gap between the Lincolns and the jets; this was to be filled by American B-29 bombers from the Mutual Defence Assistance Programme. This aircraft became the Boeing Washington B.1 in Royal Air Force service. Britain took a quantum leap, by ordering jet bombers in the shape of the Canberra, Victor, Vulcan and Valiant. As an insurance against failure of these aircraft, the Short Sperrin was ordered. The Royal Air Force did all that was asked of it, by bringing these aircraft up to a high operational standard. Squadrons of these aircraft, operating in

Bomber Command, ensured the balance of power, nuclear deterrence and the very existence of the United Kingdom.

The success of Britain's nuclear programme was on the shoulders of one individual, the brilliant William Penney. So impressed were the Americans, that they included him in much of the detail of the Manhattan Project, the race to build a nuclear bomb. Post-war, he took over all the British nuclear test programmes and succeeded in producing the British Atomic bomb. He always had an admiration for the British military, especially the Royal Air Force.

An important point arose during the later phase of the preparation of this book; looking at the Treaty of Versailles, in relation to German wartime aspirations, there is no doubt that the terms of the Treaty worked. Germany had prepared for war in 1942, but was caught early by Britain and France. Considering German technology at this time, its national development was strangled by Versailles and it was left to individuals to find any success. The German administrative apparatus was also clumsy, did not communicate and was top heavy, with nepotism putting the wrong people in the wrong job with the wrong ideas.

The development of the liquid-fuelled rocket progressed in Germany. The size and shape of supersonic and pilotless aircraft had its origins in the gliding competitions in nineteen twenties Germany, resulting in the Me163 Komet, rocket-powered fighter.

Many of the Germans who were publicly opposed to the Nazis, or made it plain that they did not support them, died in mysterious circumstances. Such was the case for Hans von Seeckt, Friedrich Sanders and Adolph Rohrbach, aircraft pioneer.

The research for "Sonic to Standoff" took place in the Mitchell Library, Glasgow, at various Glasgow archives and official places. At the time there was no electronic research; it was a search of books, reports and files. Information was received by letter, as were other enquiries. Notes were hand written and the final script was handwritten then typed. This script supported presentations. Eventually it was transferred to word processing on a disk, though not stored in file format on a computer. Eventually the script was converted into a file format and transferred to a large disk, then to a smaller disk. There was no modern software that could read this disk.

Only the paper script survived to this day, or so it was thought. The file was then found on an obsolete Apple Mac pc disk. It was then force-translated from Apple Mac format, to a Windows format which meant that it could be read by a P.C. running in a Windows environment. It was this script that formed the framework of "Sonic to Standoff."

We would like to acknowledge the help of many people who assisted in the preparation of the book, for guidance, during the early days of this project and driving it to a final conclusion. The publisher wishes to acknowledge the support and assistance of the staff of the Mitchell Library, Glasgow, in the preparation of this publication, as well as the Librarian and staff of Bishopbriggs Library. Their professionalism was of great help. Access was granted to the reports of the Aeronautical Research Committee/Council, the NACA Reports and the intelligence reports of the CIOS/FIAT/BIOS teams in Germany in 1945. To the Archivist, Librarian and staff at the University of Glasgow, the Archivist of the City of Glasgow and the Archivist of Strathclyde University, special thanks.

Many company archivists helped both here and abroad (Germany). Grateful thanks are given to the late Harry Holmes, Neil Morris, Humphry Wynn, Chaz Bowyer, Michael Channon, James Mulrine (Graphic design) and the late Walter Carter, for information, including photographs, drawings etc. and for access to official documents. Other images were provided by many ex-service personnel from private collections and are used with permission. To the Air Historical Branch of the Royal Air Force, for information and guidance and the Librarian of the Royal Aeronautical Society. To Mr J. Godwin, in the United States, for information regarding the use of heavy bombs in British and American aircraft and the joint co-operation with Tarzon. Thanks to the Aviation Bookshop, formerly Beaumont Aviation and now of Tunbridge Wells, for tracing the bibliography and providing further information etc. To Voltaire and Rousseau, Kelvinbridge, Glasgow, for supplying information, books, periodicals etc. in the bibliography and also images and to Iain Jamieson, of Jamiesons Models, for advice and encouragement. Access was given to the interviews and reports on the German war effort, many of them written by the German general staff post war

(1945-1955). Further access was given to electronic translations on a variety of relevant documents.

The German generals co-operated freely with the Allies and gave as much information as possible. Reading their reports has left a deep impression of an undercurrent of opposition to the Nazis. Sadly, lack of space, has meant that much of the personal information and anecdotes from Bomber Command and Strike Command, from squadron and personnel levels, could not be included.

Note on information and images used: N.A.R.A./Official/ USAF / Los Alamos National Laboratory*: Unless otherwise indicated, this information has been authored by an employee or employees of the University of California, operator of the Los Alamos National Laboratory under Contract No. W-7405-ENG-36 with the U.S. Department of Energy The U.S. Government has rights to use, reproduce and distribute this information. The public may copy and use this information without charge, provided that this notice and any statement of authorship are reproduced on all copies. Neither the Government nor the University makes any warranty, express or implied, or assumes any liability or responsibility for the use of this information.*

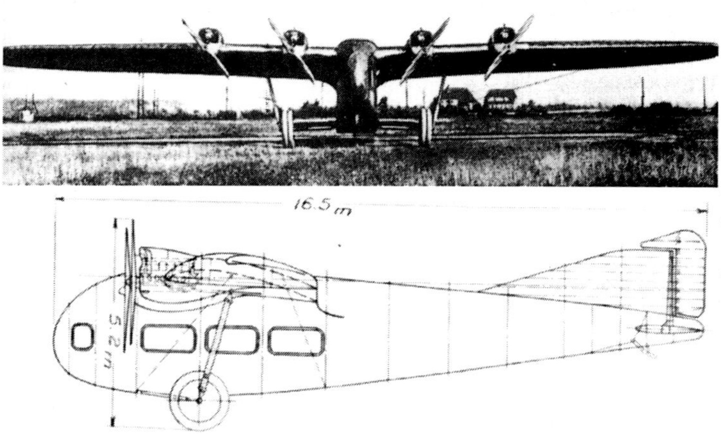

The all-metal Rohrbach , destroyed under the terms of the Versailles Treaty of 1919

Developments

During the spring of 1943, an intelligence report was circulated by the British Ministry of Aircraft Production, describing how the Luftwaffe was actively researching supersonic fighters and that Germany would have a squadron of fighters ready for operational service by June 1946. The report, gleaned from photographic reconnaissance and debriefs from captured Luftwaffe airmen, did not specify how these fighters were to be powered, nor what manufacturing company was to undertake the work, but it did give the Allies an insight into what the future specifications of fighter aircraft would be.

After the First World War, Germany was prohibited from building aeroplanes and aero - engines by the Treaty of Versailles. This treaty set up the League of Nations, gave the League its terms of reference, its secretariat and where its offices were to be situated. The treaty also set up the new borders for Germany, dismantled Austria-Hungary and included new states such as Czechoslovakia and Poland. It also guaranteed the new borders of Europe and the corridor into Danzig in Poland. The main aim of the treaty was to punish Germany for its aggression in the Great War.

The German armed forces, the Reichswehr, were to be composed of the Reichsmarine (Naval Forces) and the Reichsheer (Army Forces). Germany was to have a reduced navy, the Reichsmarine, of 10000 men, with no submarines and the army was sized at 100000. There was to be no air force, as such. The air force lasted a few months after the war as a mine clearance organisation, being reduced to 1000 men in 1919 and then was disbanded by 1920. Article 201 of the treaty set out its terms:- "*During the six months following the coming into force of the present Treaty, the manufacture and importation of aircraft, parts of aircraft, engines for aircraft and parts of engines for aircraft, shall be forbidden in all German territory.*" In accordance with the treaty obligation, the Germans handed over to the Allies 15000 aircraft and 27000 aero engines.

Aviation activities on German soil were now out of the question, since the meticulous scrutiny of the Inter-Allied Control Commission, headed by General Nollet, would have quickly found even the most insignificant effort to establish flying organizations, to produce military aircraft, or to convert civil aircraft to military uses, although in the case of Anthony Fokker, they were duped. Fokker managed to secrete over 200 airframes from the commission, sending them off on a wild goose chase and managing to get his aircraft to Holland.

Aircraft designer Anthony Fokker, on the left, post war, in Europe. He later went to America

Above, Fokker DVII fighter, which the Allies were anxious to obtain

The Inter-Allied Control Commission lasted until February 28th 1927, when the last officer was withdrawn from Germany and the Commission was dissolved.

There was one great weakness in the treaty - it did not forbid Germany from possessing or manufacturing civil aircraft. In 1922, the Commission imposed the physical size of a civil aeroplane on the German aircraft industry and what types of aircraft were allowed to be built. One major casualty of this was the giant, all-metal Rohrbach airliner, which was scrapped. By 1924, the numbers of aircraft which could be built in Germany and the size of the workforce were further laid down. This led the German aircraft industry to diversifying its manufacturing base to other European nations such as Holland (Dornier) and Denmark (Rohrbach) and in Germany former aero-engine manufacturers went on to produce car and motorcycle engines. An example of this was B.M.W. which made motorcycle engines and motor cars from the early nineteen twenties. The Paris Air Agreement of 1926 withdrew all these obligations and Germany was left a free hand in civil aviation. Immediately, the Germans expanded civil and commercial aviation with flying schools, air lines and ground training schools being formed. Under this guise, grew the foundations of a new Air Force.

Earlier, in 1920, the chief of the army, Generaloberst Hans von Seeckt, commander of the new Reichswehr, had secretly placed in the Defence Ministry 180 ex-fliers in the aeronautical sections of his department. Many of these officers, such as Kesselring, Stumpff and Sperrle, later went on to high command in the German Air Force. Von Seeckt made it perfectly clear to the Defence Ministry that the new, future air arm was to be independent of the army and navy. Von Seeckt also ignored the provisions of the Paris Air Agreement limit for personnel who were allowed to fly. In the flying schools of Deutsche Luft Hansa (the German state airline), training of military pilots was begun. A pilot of Deutsche Luft Hansa had a secondary role of that of military pilot. Luft Hansa was an amalgamation of Junkers Luftverkehr and Deutscher Aero Lloyd, becoming Lufthansa in January 1934.

In 1922, the Treaty of Rapallo was signed by Germany and the Soviet Union. Within the treaty was a secret agreement to train military pilots at a flying training centre, which was to be established at Lipetsk, in Russia. Lipetsk is situated near the Voronezh River, about 310 miles south east of Moscow. The contract to develop a flying school in Lipetsk was signed on April 15th 1925 in Moscow. It took about two years to get the facility up and running and it was only fully operational by 1927. By then, a six month training course was established for pilots. The Germans provided about fifty Fokker DXIII for training purposes and some of these were flown in Soviet markings. The Fokkers were initially packed in 50 boxes and transported by sea from Stettin to Leningrad on board the *S.S.*

Edmund Hugo Stinnes. In the summer of 1926, more aircraft were delivered for training, including two-seat "Heinkel H/D/E-17s", built in Sweden. There were initially twelve to fifteen, but by 1933 this had been reduced to seven. The base was also supplied with Junkers F.13 aircraft as couriers or transports. 1931 was the most strenuous training year, with over 300 students attending for training. Up to 1933, 120 fighter pilots graduated from the school and within the training scheme 100 observers also graduated. The observers were trained there between 1928 and 1930. 140 Russian pilots and 45 Russian aircraft mechanics were also trained there, under German supervision. Between 1930 and 1933 three students and a flight instructor were killed in flying accidents. The school was managed by Major Walter Stark, (or named in some official sources as Major Walter Schtaar), from 1925-1930, then from 1930 to 1933, by Major M. Moore and Captain G. Mueller.

Fokker D.XII fighter trainer

Heinkel "D/E 17" trainer

In addition to pilot and observer training at Lipetsk, there were also facilities for aircraft research and development, the results of which were to be made available to the Russians. At the airfield, the aircraft were initially serviced by Germans, with Russian assistance. It was found that the Russians learned quickly and the German mechanics were returned to Germany. The German and Russian flying staff and technical personnel worked closely together; the Soviet ground crews underwent training under German instructors and the Soviet fliers learned their trade from their German counterparts. The whole business was camouflaged by the Russians as "No. 4 Squadron of the Red Air Force."

There were more secret provisions in the treaty for the manufacture of aircraft by Junkers, at Fili, near Moscow. The factory at Fili only lasted until 1927, a period of slightly more than four years. There, Junkers assembled the all-metal "Ju20" and the "Ju21". It was here that the Russians learned the skill of building all-metal aircraft. The main reason that the Junkers factory failed was the lack of metal to produce airframes on site. Metal, aluminium and duralumin, were originally to be procured from the French-occupied Ruhr region of Germany. The French had discovered the true nature of the Junkers factory in Russia and the French intelligence report had been compromised by the Soviet Secret Service. The Junkers Company also wanted to build aero-engines at the site, but did not have the necessary finance or capital to build them there. Another reason for its failure was that Hugo Junkers had received grants from the German and Soviet governments to build the factory, but had diverted the funds to his plant at Dessau, in Germany.

Junkers "A.20"

Soviet "I/T-21" fighter

Inside the Junkers factory at Fili

German personnel at Fili

One of the departments set up by von Seeckt in the ministry was the "Air Technical Office". The officer in charge of this department was Captain Kurt Student, who had been one of the officers in charge of the setting up of Lipetsk. Initially, this department was organised to study technical information and gather information on aeronautical events from foreign sources and forward this information to the appropriate army department. Very early, in the formation of the Air Technical Office (1921), the department started to look at gliding in the Rhon Mountains. Earlier there had been a competition in 1920, which came to nothing and was looked upon as an experimental gliding exercise. Student organised glider flying for pilot recruits in the Deutsche Luftsportverband. One of the first glider competitions took place in September 1921, "The Rhon Soaring Competition," with 45 gliders being entered. The competition was in four categories, but there was confusion in awarding prizes for the categories, but the overall winner was Koller, in the Munich Monoplane.

In the Rhon Mountains, the Germans then fully established a separate technical department for glider research and design, being established in 1925. This research institute was called the "Rhon-Rositten Company" for glider flying at Wasserkuppe. In November 1925, Alexander Lippisch took over as its technical director. The region was located near Hanau, not far from the monastery at Fulda, north of Gersfeld in Hessen. The area was famed for its thermals and was ideal for gliding. Lippisch, together with "Bebi" Nehring, designed his first tailless glider there, named the "Storch". The Storch went through various modifications and by 1929 it was a powered glider with a maximum speed of 78 mph and a flying weight of 551 pounds. No official order was received for the Storch, because there was hostility to its tailless configuration. By 1929, Germany had succeeded in circumnavigating the terms of the Treaty of Versailles and had successfully set up eight aircraft and four aero-engine plants inside Germany. The eight aircraft plants were Albatross, Arado, Bavarian Aircraft Works, Dornier, Focke-Wulf, Heinkel, Junkers and Rohrbach. The engine plants were Argus, Junkers, Siemens and Bavarian Engine Works (Bayerische Motoren Werke, or B.M.W)

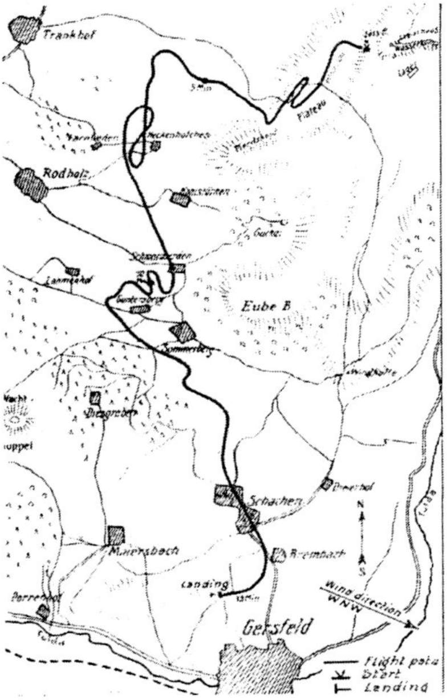

The Rhon Mountain gliding course. The competitions started here from 1920

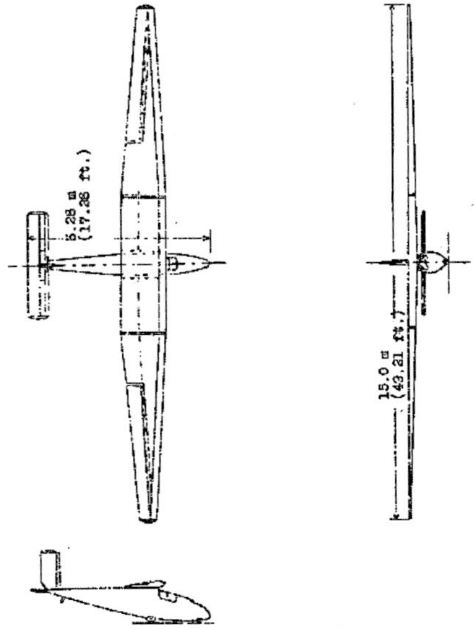

Fig.7 Hannover glider HS "Pelikan".

Hannover "Pelikan"

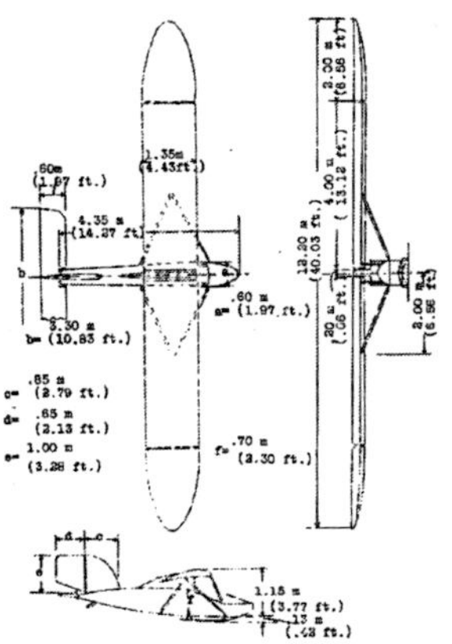

Fig.10 Dresden monoplane glider.

Dresden Monoplane Glider

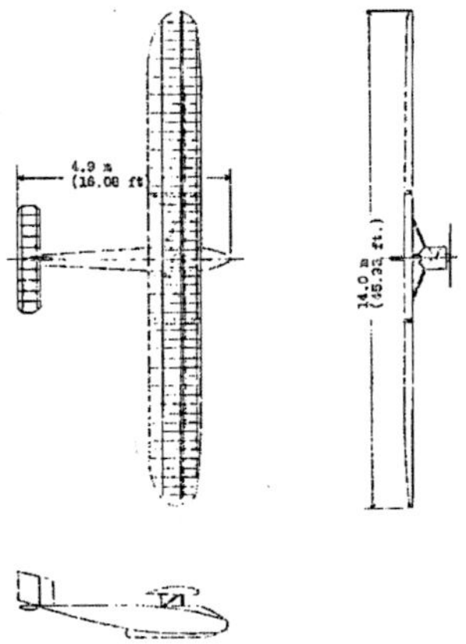

Glider "Messerschmitt" S13.

Messerschmitt Glider

It was during this period that Generaloberst Hans von Seeckt was forced to resign his appointment. In September 1926, during military manoeuvres, members of the old Imperial General Staff were allowed to be present. Also permitted to attend was the eldest son of the ex-Crown Prince, ("Clown Prince" to the wartime British Army), Prince Wilhelm. There was a storm of public protest from the Radicals and Socialists, since this was in violation of the Versailles Treaty. Von Seeckt resigned on 8th October 1926. He then went to China as a military advisor. Generaloberst Hans von Seeckt died in Berlin on 27th December 1936, under mysterious circumstances and was buried with full military honours.

Generaloberst Hans von Seeckt

Von Seeckt, a soldier with his soldiers

By 1933, Hitler had worked his magic on the German people and he had fought, bribed and coerced his way to the office of Chancellor. Along the way he picked up an ardent admirer and trusted friend in Hermann Goering. The Nazis had taken over Germany.

The flying training of pilots and observers and the testing of aircraft continued at Lipetsk until the summer of 1933, when all experiments were brought to a halt and the base closed. The Germans vacated Lipetsk by September 1933, turning over all that was left of the remaining facilities to the Soviet Union. Although the Russians were most reluctant to see the German base close, they ultimately did nothing to interfere with its closure. German officials handed over to the Soviet Union all equipment that could not be moved and everything that was not worth taking back to Germany, including all of the older Fokker D-XIIIs and Heinkels. All of the equipment, dispatched from Lipetsk, arrived safely back on German soil without any Russian interference.

There was a darker side to the closing of the Lipetsk school and the operation at Fili and German-Soviet co-operation. The majority of the Soviet staff connected with the co-operation were liquidated as spies under Stalin's purges. Personnel of the Soviet aviation detachment at Lipetsk also suffered the same fate in 1937.

"Ant 3", built using German technology

Arado on test at Lipetsk

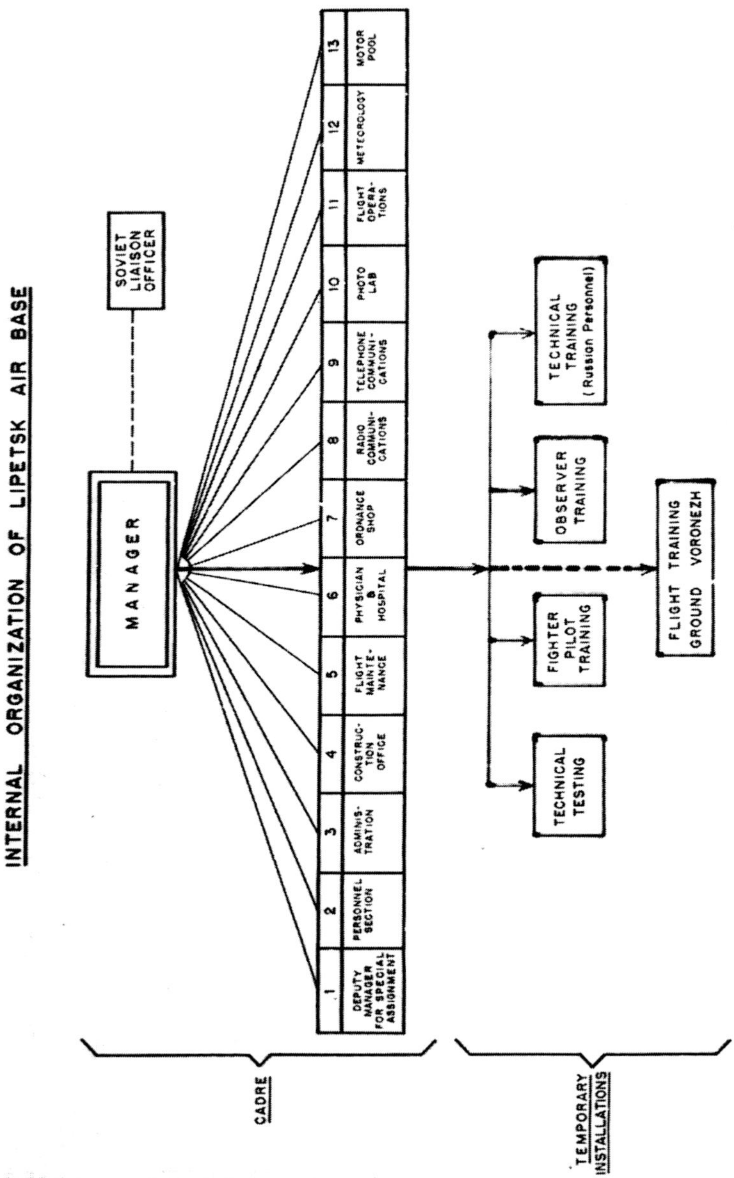

Administrative structure at Lipetsk

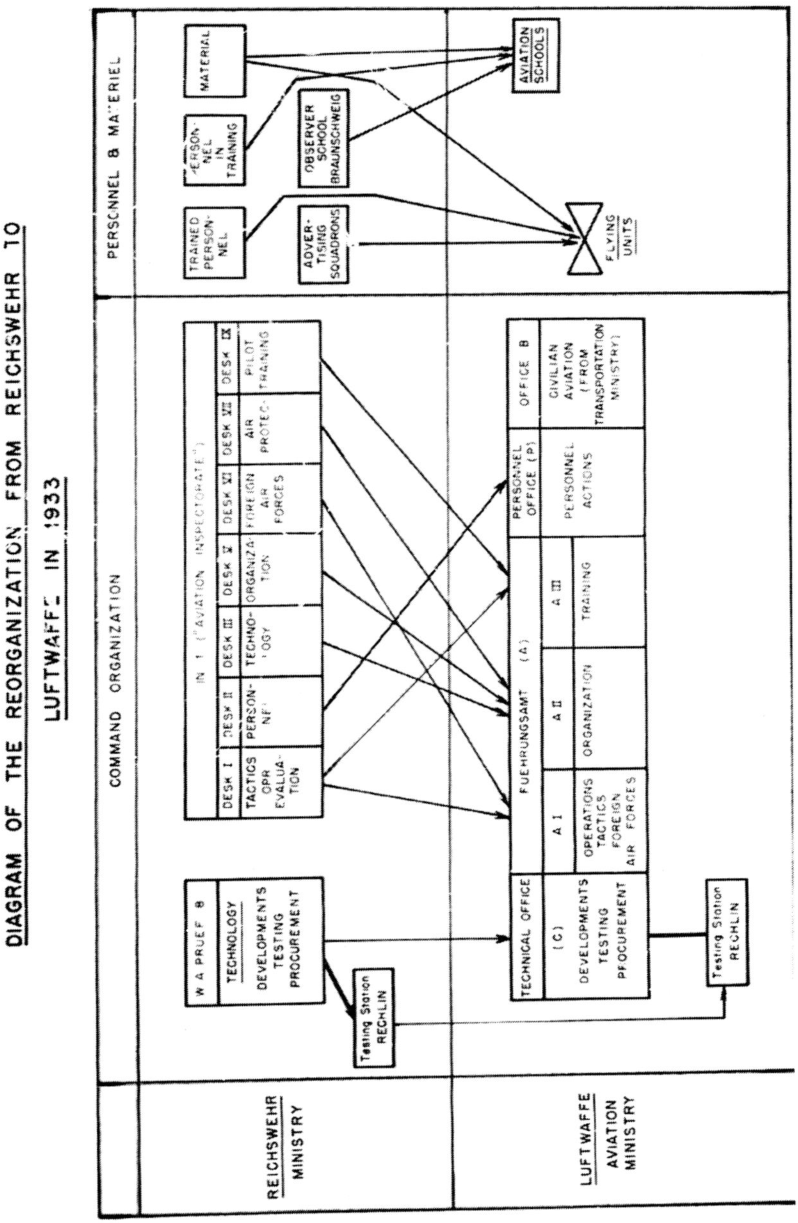

1933 transfer of Reichswehr to Luftwaffe

The Aviation Branch of the Reichswehr 1930

Front row L to R Frl. V. Marwitz, Frl. v. Mirbach, Robert Wichterich (40 years Service Anniversary,) v Zaborowski, Lambert, Schlunke, Second row Bruno Maas, Walter Schwabedissen, Fritz Loeb, Ullrich Grauert, Generalmajor Hilmar Ritter von Mittelberger, Branch Chief Hellmut Felmy, Gehrkens, Hermann; Third and Fourth Rows: Pank, Stich, v. Buellow, Morell, Giesler, v. Hollwede, Karl Drum, Werner Kreipe, Rudolf Bogatsch, v. Ledebour, v. Karmainsky

On the 1st May 1933, Germany formed the Reichs Aviation Ministry. It was divided into the Central Branch, the Air Command Office (LA), the General Air Office (LB), the Technical Office (LC), the Luftwaffe Administrative Office (LD) and the Luftwaffe Personnel Office (LP). The branches and offices were organized in the same way as those in the Reichs Defence Ministry. The Air Command Office, the most important office in the Air Ministry, was subdivided into the Operations Branch (LA-I), the Organization Branch (LA-II), the Training Branch (LA-III), the Flak Artillery Branch (LA-IV), the Supply Branch (LA-V)and the Signals Branch. A Medical Branch was also being organized at the same time. The Air Command Office and its branches, groups and important sections were all staffed with General Staff officers. For all practical purposes, the Air Command Office was the General Staff of the future Luftwaffe. The

General Air Office was the civilian office of the Ministry. The Technical Office (LC) was to deal with research, development and testing. On 15th May 1933, all German military and civilian aviation agencies were united under the Reichs Aviation Ministry, headed by the First World War fighter ace, Hermann Goering.

With the establishment of the Reichs Aviation Ministry, all of the technical agencies were consolidated under the Technical Office. Its first head was Col. Wilhelm Wiramer, who was in charge of the department. Research and development came under the command of Lt.Col. Wolfram Freiherr von Richtofen and was kept separate from procurement, which was controlled by Major Fritz Loeb, each of the departments being independent of the other. The Office Chief was in direct command of all testing, while the approval of new equipment for release to the air force was the responsibility of construction supervision specialists. The Technical Office was enlarged even more, when the Office of Supply and Procurement was established on 1st February 1939. Research, development, testing, procurement and business supervision were now all placed under the Technical Office.

After 1933, the testing stations, such as that at Rechlin, west of Stettin, not far from the Baltic coast, became more and more important. Rechlin's existence was not generally known. It was only completed after World War I and it was not accessible by any of the main transport routes. Originally, it was a testing station near Müritz Lake and had been taken over by the Reichs Defence Ministry. After 1925, it was camouflaged under the name "Testing Station Rechlin of the Reichs Formation of the German Aviation Industry." Rechlin, with its greatly enlarged plant and its increase in personnel and equipment, gradually assumed the proportions of a county rather than a research community. Rechlin had two airfields, extensive bombing and gunnery ranges, engine test beds, etc.

For the naval air units, Tarnowitz and Travemunde (the former with an island base projecting into the sea and an ideal gunnery range) remained the most important test centres. Peenemunde, originally built by the Luftwaffe, was later utilized for the building and testing of the V-weapons. Diepensee was the site of tactical experimentation. After the outbreak of war, in September 1939, it became necessary to establish aircraft test areas behind the front lines, in order to permit the testing of aircraft before release to front line units. These areas were also used for the final assembly of aircraft. In the South, lightweight aircraft were transported over the Alps by rail during periods of inclement weather and were then assembled and tested under the supervision of the Air Fleet Chief Engineer, at fields conveniently located south of the Alps.

In the beginning, these stations were directly subordinate to the Technical Office, but in 1941, in order to avoid duplication at the various establishments, the office of Commander of Testing Stations was set up under Col. Edgar Petersen. The question of whether testing stations ought to be commanded by officers or by engineers was largely one of personality. The chiefs had been able to make their opinions known to the Technical Office, to parallel agencies (industry) and to subordinate agencies (engineer and pilot personnel assigned to the stations). They needed not only to be good engineers, but excellent pilots. If they were engineers, they had to be familiar with the potentials of aircraft and operational conditions. If they were officers, they had to possess a fundamental knowledge of engineering and have a marked talent for organization. Occasionally, the Commander of Testing Sections set up special testing sections for specific projects.

Agencies concerned with basic and specialized research (Independent development companies such as Horton, Focke, Achgelis, Walter-Kassel, etc.) forwarded their findings to industry and to the Reichs Aviation Ministry. The industry was then responsible for development, construction of test models and preliminary testing, depending upon the desires of the industrial firm concerned. The testing stations intervened, either at this point, working with industrial representatives to iron out any defects as quickly as possible, or after the initial aircraft production had commenced. All equipment declared ready for introduction by the testing stations and authorized by the Reich's Aviation Ministry was then released for military testing. Aircraft from initial production, the manufacture of which had begun during the testing stage, were also assigned to the squadrons and any defects noted. These were then reported to the Technical Office, as were the subsequent corrections of those defects.

Once the tactical and technological requirements for new equipment had been determined, the Technical Office took over and worked out all the demands of the General Staff. For example, the Technical Office might disapprove of the use of a recommended material, or order the use of another, or specify what aircraft engine models were to be used. This preliminary work was followed by calling for bids on projects and awarding contracts to one or more companies. Experience had shown that it was advisable to have at least two companies working on the development of each piece of equipment.

Germany had two institutions involved in experimentation; the German Experimental Institute for Aviation in Berlin and the Experimental Institute of Aeronautics in Gottingen. The German aircraft industry felt that these two institutes were inadequate and decided to set up its own experimental station. In doing so, it failed to fund the institute correctly and the result was a duplication of efforts in research and development and a lack of leadership and direction.

The Reichs Aviation Ministry had authorized the founding of the Association for Aviation Research, an organization which was renamed on 25th June 1936 as the Lilienthal Society for Aviation Research. Its objectives, apart from the establishment of aviation research, the promotion of specialized research projects and the advancement of the exchange of scientific information, lay primarily in the area of applied technology. Additionally, the Society endeavoured to establish and maintain contact with the aviation industry, with commercial air agencies and with the authorities concerned with the administration of civilian aviation activities and to disseminate information on the latest technological advances in aviation and to promote the education of a new generation of flying enthusiasts. More ambitious research undertakings were handled by the German Academy of Aviation Research, a group which maintained contact with aviation and scientific agencies.

In 1937, the German Experimental Institute for Aviation and the Experimental Institute of Aeronautics were consolidated as the German Experimental Institute of Aviation, whose branch organizations spread rapidly from Adlershof-Gottingen to Braunschweig. This became the central research institute for aviation and entailed the following research fields:- aerodynamics, stability of construction aircraft mechanics, naval aviation activities, construction material research, engine research, manual procedures and thermodynamics, power plant mechanics, fuel research, airborne equipment and navigation and electro-physics. Goering backed the Institute with the full authority of his office and it was financed to a large extent by the Reichs Aviation Ministry. Once established, the aviation industry made no further attempt to set up research centres of its own, although a good many of the industrial research centres were, in any case, closely allied through their directors, with the official research agencies.

The Institute was handicapped by a shortage of qualified engineers (mainly because industry offered much higher salaries), as well as by the fact that Generaloberst Udet, Chief of Supply and Procurement, seemed to lack contacts among the leading personalities in the field of aviation research. At the same time, the aviation industry did not possess the required technical equipment for many undertakings and it was not until 1941, for example, that the first large-scale wind tunnels became available.

The new Luftwaffe was detached from the Reichsluftwaffe as a separate armed service on 26th February 1935. At its head was Hermann Goering, who, in an interview on 9th March 1935, announced to the world the creation of the Luftwaffe. With the announcement of the new German air force, von Seeckt's work had been fulfilled. Hitler entrusted the development of the Luftwaffe to Hermann Goering. Though an air force, separate from the control of the army was the hope of Generaloberst Hans von Seeckt, Goering had made it a reality.

The main weakness in the framework of command was Goering. It was Goering who presented all doctrine on the Luftwaffe to Hitler on a one to one basis, whether it be on research and development of aircraft, or progress on the battle front. From this, Hitler was shielded from the failures of the Luftwaffe. No technical developments could be discussed, for the simple reason that Goering was not interested, or even capable of presenting technical points.

The ignorance of both Hitler and Goering on technical matters made them both susceptible to subterfuge. A demonstration was conducted for them at the Rechlin experimental testing station on 3rd July 1939. An impressive display of Luftwaffe types was presented. They were shown rockets, rocket take-offs, new aircraft, such as the Me110 with the new 30 mm cannon, new pressurised cockpits etc. etc. Even Heinkel had been ordered to cease flight tests on his rocket powered plane, the He176, until 3rd July, so that nothing would threaten the demonstration.

The demonstration staged at Rechlin in the summer of 1939 had far reaching consequences, because Hitler and Goering possessed little detailed knowledge of the effectiveness of the Luftwaffe. All the aircraft were presented as production examples and they were told they were already rolling off the production lines. They were also shown mock air battles against obsolete aircraft, which the new aircraft easily won. None of what they saw was factual; the aircraft that they saw were not in production, or even ready for Luftwaffe squadron service. This weakness came to light after the Rechlin display and suggests that Hitler and Goering may have actually believed their own propaganda. It was simple; everything that had been shown to Hitler and Goering on 3rd July 1939 never achieved operational status until well after 1942. Major Pohle, who accompanied Hitler and Goering, made the following observations:-

"The day before, a dress rehearsal of the visit was held. During the rehearsal, Udet gave a speech, in which he mentioned each individual model and made a number of incautious predictions as to how soon each would be ready at the unit level. I immediately mentioned my reservations to Jeschonnek** and as a result, Udet was more careful the next day. Any tour of this kind has a certain fascination for the participants. Goering simply let himself be carried along by this fascination, but Hitler was not taken in to the same degree. Nevertheless, this visit to Rechlin was poison for Hitler, as well as for Goering."*

*General Udet, Chief of the Technical Office, ** Jeschonnek Chief of the Luftwaffe General Staff.

Hitler and Goering at Rechlin, examining the aircraft

The Luftwaffe's political potential mattered more and more and Hitler used it where he thought appropriate. In fact, the need to promote the Luftwaffe as a large force undermined attempts to increase its military efficacy. There was no clear doctrine in supply or strategic bombing. The manufacturers were still pursuing design philosophy, without direction. For example, Messerschmitt were pursuing production for the Bf109, while Heinkel were pressing for its replacement with the He100. Messerschmitt went on to produce giant gliders and Heinkel, the flawed He177.

Before 3rd September 1939, the Luftwaffe was sufficient in strength to make combat against each of Hitler's proposed opponents alone. In 1938, Udet and Milch visited Britain on an official visit, which in reality was an inspection of the Royal Air Force. In Milch's report he pointed out that there was deterioration in diplomatic protocols between Germany and Britain. Milch felt that this had been caused by the conduct of the German Ambassador, Ribbentrop. With the looming crisis of Danzig and Czechoslovakia, Milch warned Hitler that Britain would go to war on these issues and it would be a mistake for Germany, not yet fully re-armed, to provoke war. The role of the Luftwaffe had not yet crystallised by 1939, but it was the same situation worldwide - ideas on air power were at an experimental stage. If everything had gone to plan then the pre-war theories of the German General Staff would have proved sound enough. But this war was not to be a quick war and it found the Luftwaffe very weak in four-engined bombers and night fighters and in home defence doctrine. It could be said that the tactical support of the army until 1941 proved the effectiveness of air power and that the Luftwaffe had adhered to its pre-war theories up to that time. But, after 1941, it was completely different.

The British and French declarations of war on 3rd September 1939, marked the end of Hitler's policy to defeat his opponents, one by one. Intrinsically the Luftwaffe was too weak to fight two opponents at the same time, but the image of an invincible Luftwaffe, ready to wage war for the Fuhrer and Germany, was allowed to continue.

Pioneering the Rocket

Despite the success of military rockets from the middle of the 18th century, they lost their significance during the second half of the 19th century, because of the introduction of rifling in infantry weapons and barrel artillery, which increased their accuracy. Rockets had all but disappeared from the military inventory by the 1880s. However, the idea of rocket flight still persisted and appeared in the subsequent writings of various inventors. The father of modern rocket propulsion was the American, Dr. Robert Hutchings Goddard. Along with Tsiolkovsky of Russia and the Rumanian-born Oberth of Germany, Goddard clearly saw the exploration of space through rockets. By 1926, Goddard had constructed and successfully tested his first rocket, using liquid fuels. The rocket was launched by Goddard and flew 56 metres in 2.5 seconds. The flight of Goddard's rocket on March 16th, 1926, at Auburn, Massachusetts, was a feat as epoch-making as that of the Wright Brothers at Kitty Hawk in 1903. Primitive in their day, as was the achievement of the Wright Brothers at Kitty Hawk, Goddard's rocket successes made little impression upon the America public or American government officials.

In 1916, Goddard wrote an essay requesting funds so that he could continue his research. This essay was later published, along with his subsequent research, in "Smithsonian Miscellaneous Publication No. 2540 (January 1920)". It was entitled, "A Method for Reaching Extreme Altitudes." Like all Smithsonian publications, it was freely available to the rest of the scientific world. Upon request, in 1922, Goddard sent an autographed copy to Hermann Oberth of Germany and received a warm letter of thanks from the early German pioneer of rocketry. Oberth's publication in Germany, in 1923, of "Die Rakete zu den Planetenraumen (Rocket into Planetary Space)" gave new life to the Russian Tsiolkovsky's basic theory of rocket propulsion, which had been proposed in 1898. Oberth's book also elaborated, in greater detail, the application of rocket propulsion to spaceflight, even proposing an artificial satellite going into orbit around the Earth.

Rockets in China

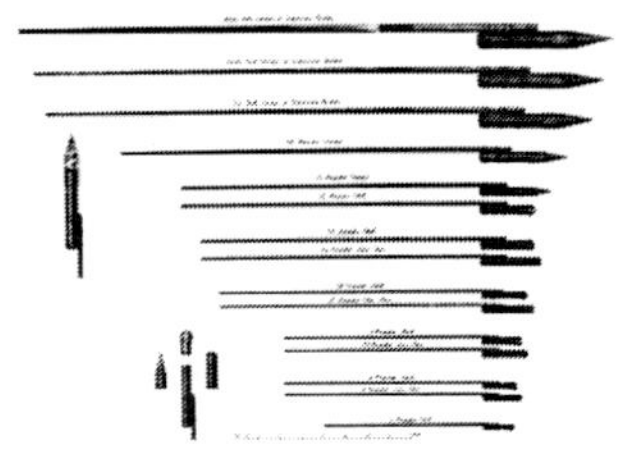

British Congreve rockets

Robert Goddard with his first rocket

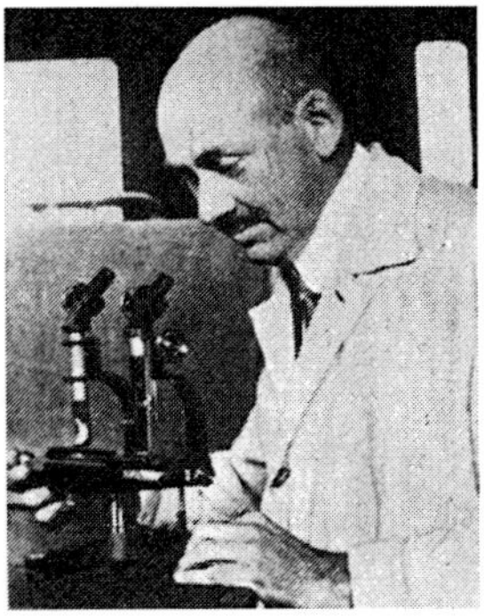

Rocket pioneer Robert Goddard

Konstantin I. Tsiolkovsky

Hermann Oberth

Oberth believed that passengers could travel to and from the satellite in smaller “landing rockets”. In this way, the satellite could be transformed into a manned space station, which could ultimately serve as a launching point for spacecraft. Neither Goddard nor Oberth mentioned the possible use of rockets as military weapons.

In Russia, the idea of rocket flight was put forward in the works of Russian scientist, Konstantin I. Tsiolkovsky. In 1903, the journal “Science Review” (“Nauchnoye Obozreniye”) published his scientific work, “The Investigation of Space Using Rocket Devices,” where he first pointed to the rocket as a means of interplanetary flight, mentioned methods for mastering outer space and gave the basic laws of rocket flight. In his first article he worked out the idea of liquid-fuelled rockets. His rocket fuel was a mixture of oxygen and hydrogen as propellants, a compound for engine cooling and the use of pumps to force-feed fuel to the engine. In the 1920s Tsiolkovsky's ideas received universal recognition and by 1929 he had the idea of constructing multi-stage rockets or, as he called them, “rocket trains.”

One of the great myths that came out of the First World War was that the Germans had been using rocket shells. There were un-substantiated accounts of rocket shells being used with a German long-range gun of 1918. This gun, called “La Parisienne” by its German gun troop, fired around 320 rounds into the city of Paris. Although information on this gun was scarce at the time, all the available reports indicated that the shells were thrown into the stratosphere not only by the propellant charge, but also by a rocket-device attached to the bottom of the shell. When the gun was fired the trajectory of the shell reached a height of 24 miles at a speed of 2200 feet per second and when it struck the ground, it had a velocity of 2450 feet per second. The barrel was 120 feet long and was supported by a cradle. The gun was designed by Dr Otto von Eberhard and Dr Fritz Rausenberger of Krupp, both physicists, who had persuaded General Ludendorff that a gun with a 60 mile range could be built. To increase the range further, a smooth-bore barrel was added to the end of the rifled barrel. When first tested, all the shells failed and the rounds had to be redesigned. The modified shells were screwed into the barrel at the breech and when fired, spun at 107 revolutions per

The German gun, "La Parisienne", of 1918

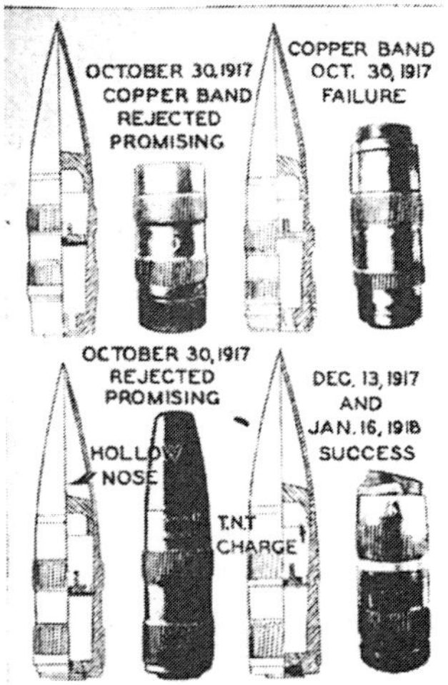

Test rounds for the Paris Gun. The round marked "54" was the finalised design. The nose was screwed into the body.

second. The shell was enormously thick and was fitted with two fuses and caused massive barrel wear. The Allies never proved that the shell was rocket-assisted, because they never found an example to inspect. The guns, between five and eight in number, were spirited away by the Germans after the Armistice and broken up. The use of the Paris gun, firing shells into the upper atmosphere, introduced the effect of gravity and atmosphere to the military and the scientists. These shells were the first man-made objects fired into the edge of space. During this period, 1918, experiments were also being made with rocket-assisted seaplanes, in the Baltic.

The pioneer of private German rocket research was Fritz von Opel, the German automobile manufacturer, but his interest in rocket development was only for the publicity value that it would give his automobile company. In 1928, some ten years from the end of the war, Opel first showed in public his rocket-propelled car. Several types were made and from the largest version a speed of 146 mph was obtained. Opel supplied a solid-fuel rocket motor, to be fitted to a prototype glider called the "Ente". This rocket glider had three successful flights, but on its third flight one of the rockets exploded and set the glider on fire. Opel was disappointed with the result of this work and when he heard that a student, Julius Hatry, was planning to build another glider and install a battery of solid fuel Sanders rockets under the tail, he promptly bought the design and promised the student a gratuity if it was a success. (Friedrich Sanders was ably assisted at this time by Max Valier, a member of the Verein fur Raumschiffart, on these trials.) With Opel at the controls, the first flight took place at Frankfurt-Rebstock on 30th September 1929, but with so much thrust available, the glider became unstable and difficult to fly. The student never got his gratuity. It was obvious that the Germans had to do much more research into the rocket glider and many models were tested with a variety of power plants to see if a rocket plane was viable.

In April 1930 Captain Walter Dornberger was assigned to the Ordnance Branch of the army's Ballistics and Weapons Office to work on rocket development at the Kummersdorf firing range, fifteen

The Ente rocket glider, designed by Alexander Lippisch

Opel, with the first rocket plane

Sanders and Opel

The Opel-Sanders Rak1 in flight and flight preparation.

miles south of Berlin. During World War I Dornberger had been an artillery officer working on the Paris Gun. The German Army's first official act, in regard to the development of rockets, was a conference of officers at the Army Ordnance Office on 17th December 1930. At this conference, the work of all the civilian engineers and scientists in the field was reviewed. A powder rocket projector, developed in Sweden in early 1900, was discussed in detail, as were the experiments of Dr Goddard. The conference agreed to push the development of rockets further and to allocate the equivalent of fifty thousand dollars from Ordnance Funds. The first year of the Army's support saw sufficient progress for the Chief of the Army Ordnance Office to approve the allotment of another $50000 for the project. By 1st August 1932, the organizational set-up for research and development was formed. Research Station West, under Dornberger, included three pioneering engineers and scientists, who had been at Kummersdorf.

A solid-fuelled powder rocket, which was an improvement on the early Swedish model, had been developed and the feasibility of liquid rocket propulsion had been sufficiently proved to Captain Dornberger to justify further experimentation.

When the National Socialist (Nazi) Party came to power in 1933, Germany decided to investigate the use of the rocket as a practical power unit, as a matter of policy. To develop this new propulsion unit for the Luftwaffe, a department, under the leadership of Dornberger, was formed by the Air Protection Branch of the Reichluftfahrt-Ministcrium (German Air Transport Ministry). This new department was quickly installed in the former headquarters of the Deutsche Rakete Gesellschaft, D.R.G. (German Rocket Society) at Tempelhof Aerodrome, on the outskirts of Berlin. Some other sources describe the society as Verein fur Raumschiffart (V.F.R.). (This German Rocket Society had been formed in Berlin in 1927.) The German word used for absorption of a private body by the state was "*Gleichschaltun*". This word was used for the process by which all organisations and associations, existing in German society, were Nazified and some, such as the political parties and the trade unions, were simply suppressed. The D.R.G. had been effectively and completely Nazified.

Max Valier, a member of the V.F.R who had helped Opel with his rocket experiments and was the first pilot to fly a rocket-powered aircraft, was considered somewhat of an outsider by the D.R.G., because he confined his initial activities to solid-fuel rockets, which were outside the limits of the Society. Valier lost his life, when one of his liquid rocket car engines exploded under test in January 1930, as he was filling the fuel tank, hurling him 20 feet into the air. When he was placed inside the ambulance, it was found that he had already passed away.

This rocket society is worthy of note, because nearly all their early research work was on liquid-fuel rockets and had been carried out by members of the D.R.G., under the leadership of Hermann Oberth. These experimenters set up a testing ground on the edge of Tempelhof, which they called the Raketeflugplatz (Rocket Aerodrome) and from here a number of early, successful test rockets were fired.

Willy Ley was also vice-president of the German Rocket Society. He became the world's most popular author on the subject of rockets, missiles and space travel, or science-fiction. The society began at once to experiment with liquid-fuelled rocket engines. The rockets carried two tanks, one gasoline and one of liquid oxygen. These two liquids had to be fed simultaneously and in the right proportions to the combustion chamber, where they were mixed and burned. Most of the early launchings ended in failure, for two reasons; firstly, liquid oxygen is extremely cold and froze the valves, so that they refused to open or close at the proper time. Secondly, the combustion temperature was so high that the rocket burned up after a few seconds. In later experiments, the combustion chamber was surrounded by a cooling jacket filled with water. With this model, the society launched a number of rockets that burned for about thirty seconds and reached an altitude of half a mile or more. The next step was to omit the water from the cooling jacket and circulate the fuel through the jacket, before burning it. When the society tried to launch such a rocket, using gasoline as a fuel, it immediately exploded. Ley suggested using

Max Valier in his Rocket Car

Valier with early German liquid-fuelled rockets under test

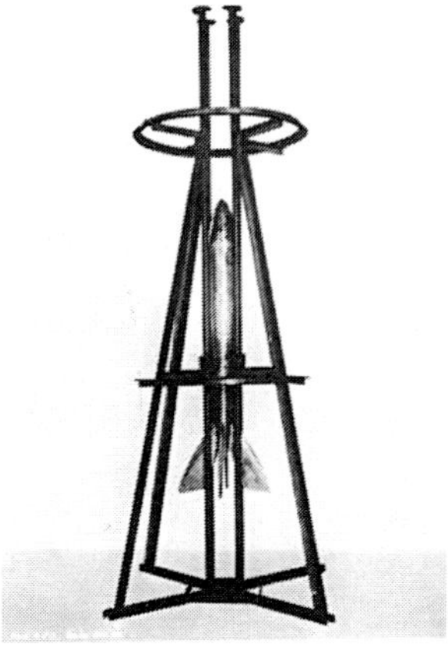

Testing Oberth's early rocket

Fuelling Max Valier's rocket car

ethyl-alcohol, slightly diluted with water, in place of gasoline. This system worked very well. In the early part of 1933, the department under Walter Dornberger was again reorganized and transferred to Peenemunde-Karlshagen. This new research establishment was first named Heeresversuchsanstalt Peenemunde (Army Research Institute, Peenemunde), but was later was renamed the Heimat Artillery Park. Initially, this experimental centre was divided into two sections, one dealing with test-bed work and manufacturing facilities (being controlled by the German Army) and the other section dealing with all flight test work (supervised by the German Air Force). Under the direction of Dornberger they were to develop liquid-fuelled rockets for use as weapons. Nobody in Germany had any experience with rocket propulsion, apart from members of the Society for Space Travel, so Dornberger visited the society and hired a very young member named Werner von Braun. The team of Dornberger and von Braun, with a small staff of assistants, began to test rocket motors on an artillery testing range near Berlin. In this same year Werner von Braun developed the army's first stabilized liquid fuelled rocket, called the Aggregate 2 (A2), which was successfully launched in 1934.

Professor Helmuth Walter, a prominent engineer-chemist, who had served in the German Navy in the Great War, formed a company, called Helmuth Walterwerke, Kiel, (H.W.K.), to develop and manufacture rocket-power units. Walter had previously designed a wakeless marine torpedo propulsion unit, using hydrogen-peroxide as fuel. The chief product of the decomposition of this fuel was steam, which rapidly condensed in the water, leaving no wake. Before the war, an 80-ton experimental submarine was built at Kiel and demonstrated a submerged speed of 25-26 knots. This submarine had an H.W.K experimental motor and was followed, during the Second World War, by four training boats and five operational boats, designated as type 17B. These had a 380-ton displacement, surface speed of 8.5 knots and submerged speed of 25 knots. However, they were never put into operational use because of the shortage of hydrogen peroxide.

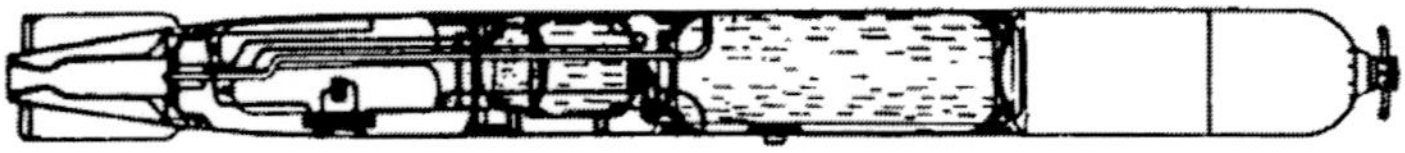

Underwater power plant LT 1500, T-B-Z-substance, 800 kilograms, 60 seconds.

The Helmuth Walter torpedo

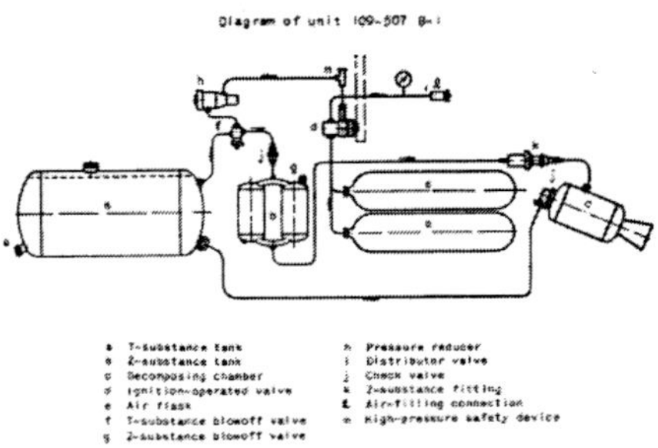

Early Walter flying bomb motor - 1937

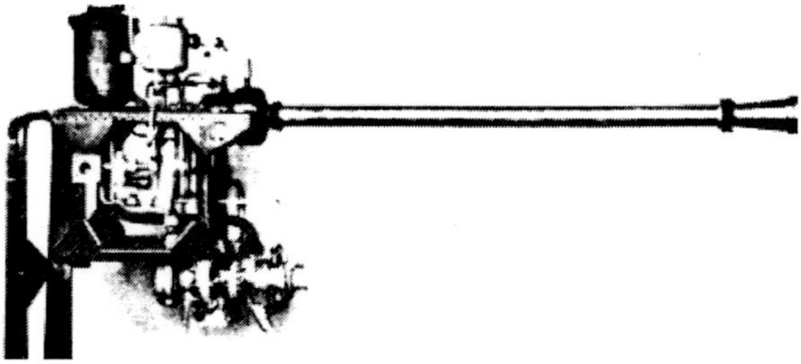

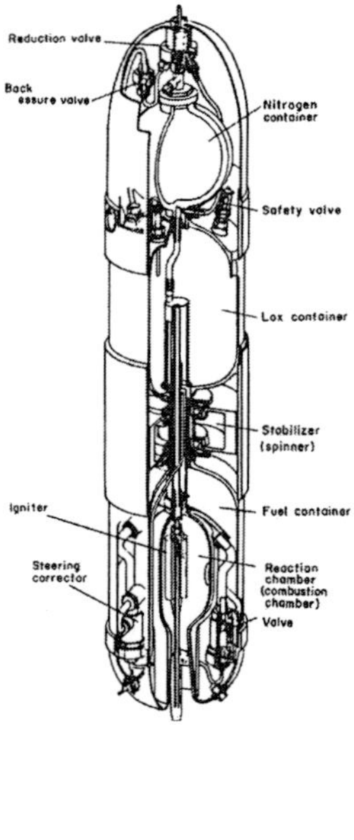

Prototype H.W.K. rocket motor, above

To the right, von Braun's A2

The German Air Ministry requested a similar H.W.K. experimental motor for the assisted-take-off of aircraft. By 1936, a successful assisted take-off unit had been manufactured and was tested by the Deutches Versuchsanstalt für Luftfahrt (German Research Institute for Air Travel) at Berlin-Adlershof. In 1936, Walterwerke, Kiel received a contract to design and build a rocket-propulsion unit to power a high-speed aeroplane (later known as the D.F.S.194), which was being designed by Professor Alexander Lippisch. To flight-test this Walter rocket motor, the specially-designed Heinkel He176 was employed during 1936-37. The Heinkel He176 was a single-seat all-metal monoplane with a fixed undercarriage. Numerous high-speed ground runs were carried out with the He176, but the Walter unit developed insufficient thrust to get the aircraft airborne, compounded by the fact that the He176 had an extremely high wing-loading, by the standards of the day. It did eventually achieve flight, on 20th June 1939, but this only lasted fifty seconds. The He176 project was considered a failure and abandoned.

Trials of the rocket motor continued and at one stage, a He112 had a unit fitted in the tail, as a booster for the piston engine.

Taking heed of the official interest in jet propulsion, the Heinkel concern, Ernst Heinkel Aktiengesellschaft, commenced experiments on gas turbines in 1936, at the newly acquired Hirth Motoren Werk G.m.b.h., situated at Stuttgart/Zuffenhausen. Experiments were conducted under the guidance of Dr. Ing. Schif, the Technical Director of Heinkel-Hirth and several units were constructed. In late 1938, ground runs took place with the specially designed flying test-bed, the Heinkel He 178, fitted with the first Heinkel flight-test gas turbine, the He S 3. These tests, conducted at Rechlin, culminated in the world's first flight by a jet-propelled aircraft, on August 27th, 1939

In 1935 a new research plant had been opened to investigate all types of glider and powered flight, the Deutsche Forschungsanstal fur Segelflug (D.F.S.). The glider section was divided into two parts - the first part was concerned with the conventional glider, while the second part was formed to investigate tailless and all-wing gliders. Powered by a 75 h.p. Pobjoy radial, the D.F.S.39 Delta IVc was designed by Alexander Lippisch and was a tandem two-seat tailless monoplane, which gained its full German C of A in 1936. At the turn of 1937, Dr. Lorenz, assistant research director at the German Air Ministry, asked Lippisch to redesign the D.F.S.39 around a Walter liquid rocket engine. At the D.F.S., this project was called Project X. Before construction of an aeroplane commenced, a series of tests were conducted around wind tunnel and free flight models. While these tests into Project X were taking place, another parallel development was under study, this being the D.F.S.194, a tailless glider powered by a 100 h.p. Argus engine, driving a pusher airscrew. When war broke out in 1939, the 194 was shelved, in order to concentrate on other designs. As 1940 closed, the design of the D.F.S.194 was changed from a piston-engined, research plane to a single-engined rocket-powered experimental glider. First flight tests of the D.F.S. 194 rocket-propelled fighter were carried out with a conventional aero-engine and propeller, although later tests of the prototype D.F.S. 194 were carried out with a Walter liquid-fuelled rocket unit. The development of the D.F.S.194 was shrouded in secrecy and involved many who were to become famous rocket engineers in later years, including Werner von Braun, who had been closely involved with Heinkel rocket fighters in 1937. These rocket tests were carried out at Peenemunde and when the 194 was flown under test the performance exceeded all expectations, one flight being recorded at 342 mph. The test pilot on these occasions was Heini Dittmar and in July 1941 he performed the first rocket motor trial at Peenemunde, with the Walter II-203b rocket engine. The success of these tests really got the German Air Ministry enthusiastic about the rocket plane and they asked Messerschmitt to design a point defence rocket interceptor, which was to become the Me163B Komet. Lippisch was then invited to join the Messerschmitt concern at Augsburg, where the aircraft was to go into quantity production.

An He112 of the type used in rocket tests. The motor was fitted to the tail

Heinkel's first jet, the HE178

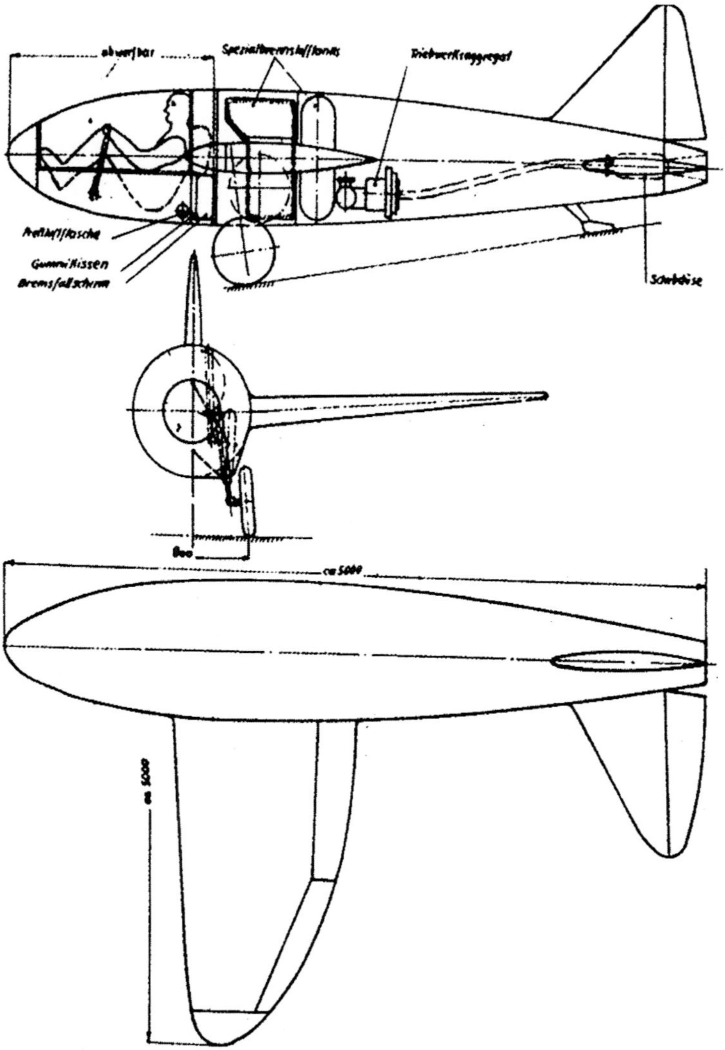

A 1954 impression of the He176, lacking a nose wheel and different tail detail from the original.

The first tailless glider, "Storch 1"

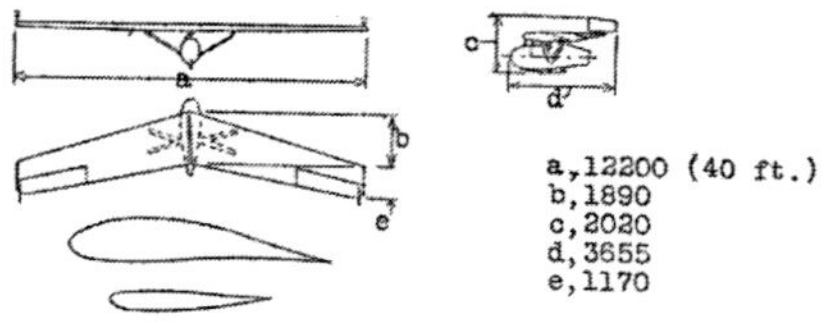

Test glider model "Storch" first form, 1927.

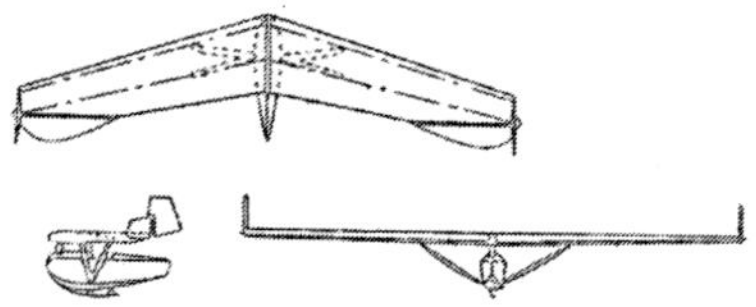

"Storch" glider.

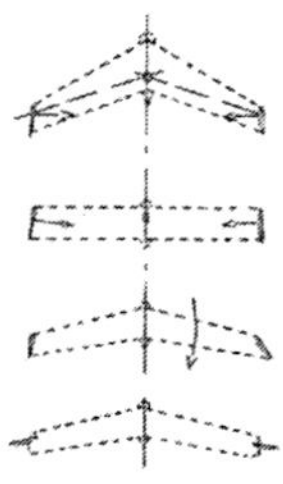

Operation of lateral rudders.

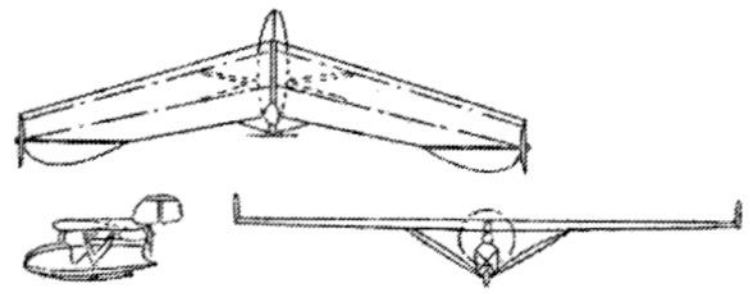

Light tailless airplane "Storch" equipped with DKW 7-9 hp engine.

The Storch series of gliders and the powered, Storch IV

Storch IV takes off

Three-quarter view of the Dreieck I airplane showing ailerons and wing-tip rudders.

Storch IV engine installation

Lippisch mail carrier

D.F.S. 39 Delta IVC

The problems for the German Air Ministry now started in earnest. The first production rocket fighter had been designed around the D.F.S.194 and was to be built by two companies, Messerschmitt and Heinkel; the latter was to build the wings, while the former was to build the fuselage. Serious trouble erupted when the two companies refused to work with each other and as a result Messerschmitt took over all development of the 194. For Messerschmitt, the D.F.S.194 became the Messerschmitt 163, still with their code name Schwalbe (Swallow), not Komet. Komet was an obvious and apt nickname for this rocket - propelled fighter, which came into use when, as a fighter, it entered service.

However, the results for the D.F.S.194 were far more satisfactory than with the Heinkel aeroplane, the maximum speed attained being 350 mph with an initial climbing speed of 5,300 ft. per min. A direct result of the success of the D.F.S.194 was the fact that Prof. A Lippisch was invited by a director of Messerschmitt Aktieng-esellschaft, Augsburg, to join this company and continue his experimental and practical work. First flight tests were completed at the Heimat Artillery Park (H.A.P.) experimental establishment at Peenemunde, using the Me163a as a glider, although later tests were carried out with the Walter H.W.K. 509 (109-509) rocket unit installed. In all, ten Me163a Schwalbe fighters were built and tested — but not without loss of life.

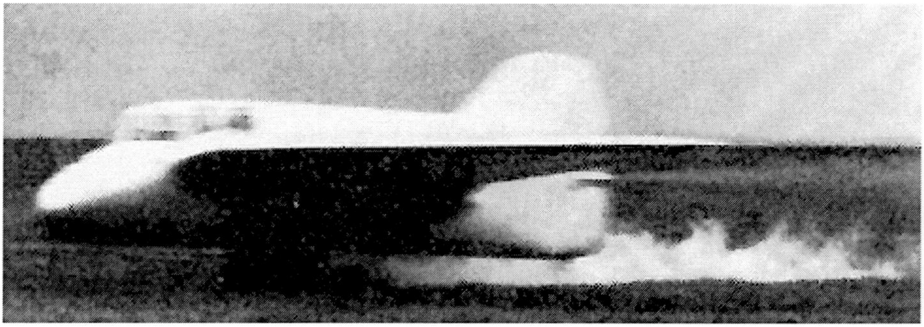

D.F.S. 194

In the first stages of 163 development with the H.W.K. motor, a simple power plant, utilizing the decomposition of concentrated hydrogen peroxide alone was used. However, the specific impulse of this system was quite low and it was replaced by a bi-propellant "hot" unit, using a fuel consisting of a mixture of 30% hydrazine hydrate plus dissolved catalyst (potassium copper cyanide), 57% methyl alcohol and 13% water. This fuel was self-igniting with hydrogen peroxide. Methyl alcohol was used in the fuel mixture to extend the supplies of hydrazine-hydrate and water was added to reduce the combustion temperature. The aircraft weighed 4200 pounds when fully-fuelled and the rocket motors could produce 2300 pounds of thrust, which enabled it to climb to 30000 feet in about two minutes. Even though 49% of the take-off weight of the aircraft was propellant, its operational radius was extremely limited and it had a normal endurance of only 10 to 20 minutes at most. The fuel supply was sufficient for only 4 minutes at the maximum rate of consumption.

Following the death, in 1941, of General Ernst Udet, director of the research and experimental establishments of the German Air Force, all testing stations were reorganized. The H.A.P. at Peenemunde-Karlshagen, the Marine Aircraft Centre at Travemunde and the Aircraft Armament Centre at Tarnewitz, were brought under the direct control of the main experimental station at Rechlin. The importance of this move cannot be under-estimated, as all the research work on German aircraft was, at once, completely centralized and co-ordinated, instead of being scattered. Following the partial success of the Messerschmitt Me163a Schwalbe, during trials in 1941, the German Air Ministry placed an order for a limited number of a modified version, to be designated the Me163b. The prototype airframe was completed in 1942, but powered flights were not attempted until the following year. In the Me163b, the Walter H.W.K. 509 (or 109-509) "hot" unit was employed, using a mixture of hydrogen-peroxide and hydrazine-hydrate-methyl-alcohol as fuel.

Towards the end of 1943, Professor A. Lippisch was forced to leave Messerschmitt, Augsburg, because of political pressure

Early Me163 prototypes and the H.W.K .motor installation

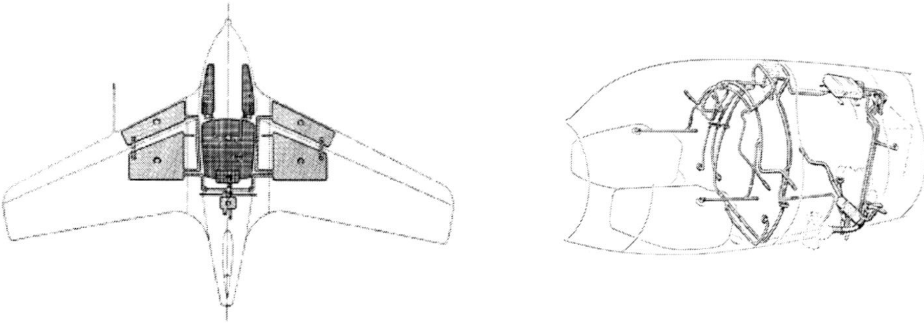

Me163 fuel tank arrangements

brought to bear by Professor Messerschmitt, who had long regarded Professor Lippisch as an "unwanted intruder." The German Air Ministry were not happy with progress on the 163 and as a direct result, wanted all production of the Me163 Schwalbe to be handed over to the Junkers Flugzeugbau concern of Dessau. Nevertheless, a later Junkers-designed variant of the Me163 appeared, complete with tricycle undercarriage, a Walter H.W.K.509c rocket unit and an improved all-round performance, designated the Junkers Ju248 and sometimes known as Ju263 or 8-263.

Germany also supplied technical assistance to its eastern ally, Japan. A captured file of Elektrochemischen Werke, Munchen manufacturers of liquid-rocket chemical fuels, contained documents which indicated a strong probability that plans for the Walter H.W.K. 109-509 power unit of the Me163 had arrived in Japan. Contained in that file was a letter, dated 9th August 1944, from Walter's Berlin office, which quoted a 13th July order from the German Air Ministry to manufacturers of jet and rocket-aircraft and power units that delivery of drawings should take place, regardless of the signing of agreements covering manufacturing rights. Walter's letter continued with the statement that the Walter factory at Kiel had already delivered to the Japanese in Berlin all drawings, including ten sets of plans and a complete plan of the works. It is possible that the drawings and an aircraft were handed over to Japanese representatives in Berlin on 13th July, the date on which those representatives received all drawings in connection with the manufacture of liquid rocket chemical fuels. Since there were ten copies, at least one set of drawings for the Walter H.W.K. 109-509 had arrived in the Far East by the end of the year.

Further information was given to the Japanese in regard to the use of beech plywood for the mainplanes and on thicknesses of the skin at various points along the wing. Information on the adhesives used for the wooden parts of the aircraft, the process for manufacturing main wing spars and laminated wing surfaces and the repair of wings was also provided. In September-October the Japanese representatives first learned some detail of the Me163C. Tokyo nevertheless attempted to build at least an experimental copy of the Me163 on the basis of the information available from Germany and anticipated operations at some future date. Also found in Japan was evidence of a Japanese request for information on Me163 tactics and German methods of ground control. It seems clear that Japan appreciated the possibilities of the Me163 as a defensive weapon against B-29 attacks, where its high rate of climb would be of the greatest value. While its limited endurance was disadvantageous, against this must be weighed the fact that many of Japan's primary targets for air attack were in coastal areas. With limited radar warning, a fast-climbing fighter was essential. Also, the use of an aircraft powered by chemical fuels would help alleviate a tight aviation fuel situation. It is probable, therefore, that strenuous efforts were made to produce the Me163 in Japan. Although no sample aircraft and probably no complete set of blueprints for the aircraft arrived in the Far East, the information available was probably sufficient to allow an attempted construction of the aircraft. Apparently, however, the experiments were not successfully completed. No positive identification of the Me163 was reported by combat crews operating over Japan, nor were any identified on photographic cover. One example, however, was found by a U.S. Navy inspection group at Yokosuka.

Armed with twin 30 mm cannon, the Me163 proved a potent interceptor and bomber destroyer in Europe, but its main disadvantage was its short endurance and limited flight envelope. There was also the problem of unburnt fuel remaining in the tanks. This was highly volatile and 80 percent of losses of the 163 type were due to this mixture exploding on landing. Such was the economy of design in this little fighter, that it lacked any undercarriage; it used a twin, jetisonable bogie for take-off and a single skid for landing. On occasion the twin bogie could bounce up after dropping and hit the aircraft. This system had been proved in tests with the D.F.S.194, but it had one great weakness; the position of the skid was critical on landing and care had to be taken to select the correct setting. If it was set too high the skid would hit the ground with a severe jolt, dislodge the pilot's seat and the fuel tanks thus detonating any remaining fuel. But even with all these difficulties, connected with airframe design and pilot survivability, the Walter engine went on to power missiles with a completely different mission profile from that of point air defence.

Me163 take-off

An Me163, captured by the British, on display in London and at an RAF base

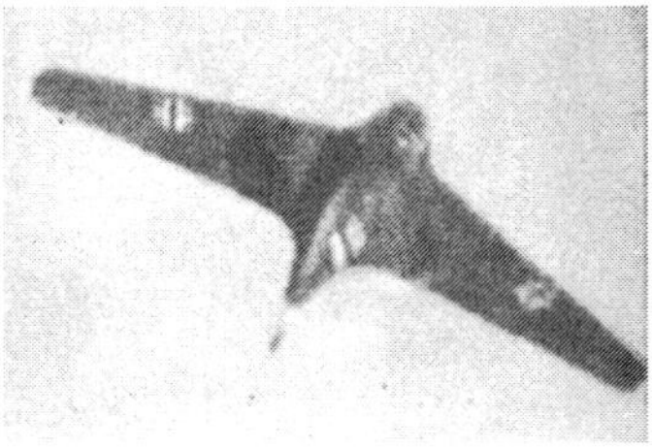

Captured Me163 *Komet in flight*

Heavily modified Junkers Me263

Japanese-built Me163, the Mitsubishi J8M Shūsui

Japanese ME163 training gliders

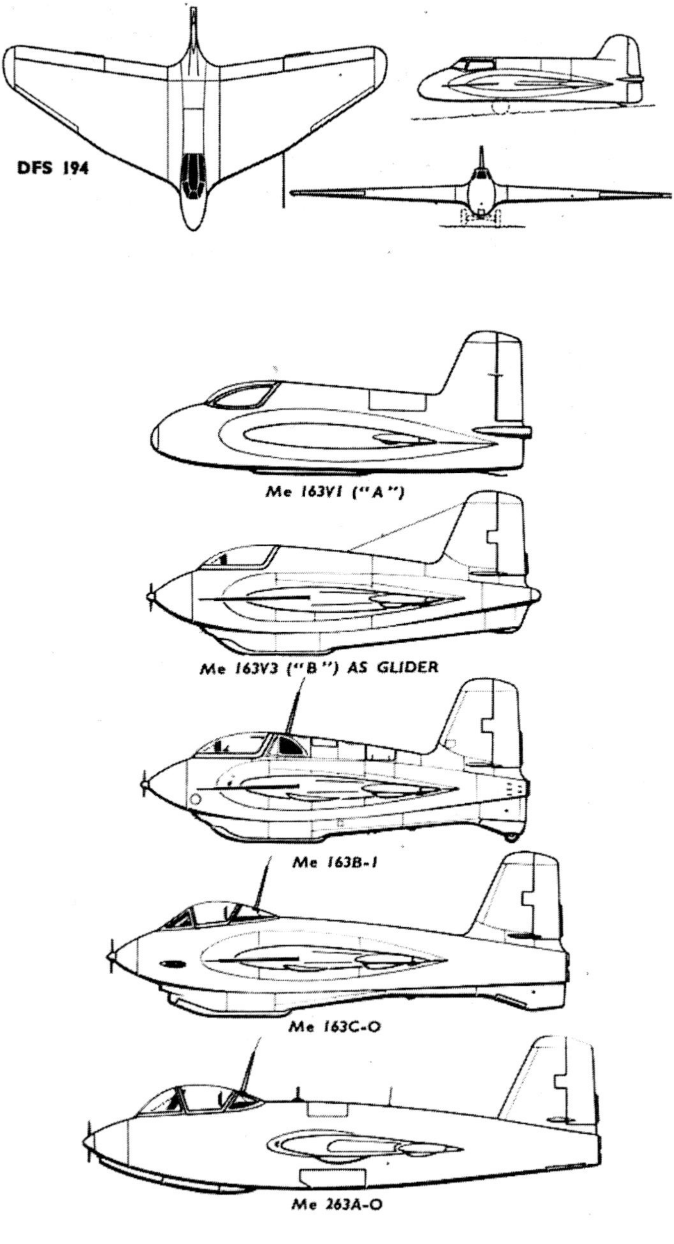

Genesis of the Me163 Komet rocket fighter (1954 official)

Spy Planes

As work on the new rocket fighters was progressing, the D.F.S. organisation was tasked with the development and construction of a new design, the D.F.S. 228. This aircraft was of revolutionary design, being nothing more than a rocket-propelled sailplane. It was built to a 1941 specification, for an extremely high altitude reconnaissance aircraft, which would use a rocket motor for take-off and resort to soaring flight, to obtain its range. Much experienced in designing high -altitude sailplanes, Felix Kracht was responsible for the D.F.S. 228. In 1939, Kracht's team had designed a sailplane which had flown to 38000ft, with a pilot using oxygen and they had concluded that, at such limits, the aircraft required a pressure cabin. The prototype D.F.S. 228 was registered D-IBFQ and it was built in three sections; nose pressure cabin, fuselage centre section and a tail cone. The wing was all-wood, with wooden ribs and plywood covering. The wooden centre section was designed with twin skids, camera bay, fuel tanks and rocket motor. The D.F.S.228 had a length of 34ft 7in, a wingspan of 57ft 6in and weighed 9270lbs. In the prototype, the pilot sat in a cartridge-operated ejection seat for flight tests at low altitudes. In later versions, the pilot lay on a couch, in the prone position, in a Plexiglas nose, which was attached to the rear bulkhead, while the wooden structure was insulated by a layer of aluminium foil between the inner and outer shells. For pilot entry, the nose could slide about three feet forward, allowing the pilot to enter the pressure cabin. Pressurisation could only be maintained up to 26000ft and above this altitude compressed air bottles had to be used. The pilot had another piece of ingenuity, to help maintain pressure; his breath was used and as he exhaled, it was dried, before being allowed into the cabin's atmosphere. An oxygen system was included and this was more unusual than the breath-drying system. A tube was fitted into the fuselage, through which cold air was passed and slow burning cartridges heated the air. The motor for the D.F.S.228 was identical to the Me163, a Walter 109-509a, with the twin fuel tanks in the fuselage centre section. For operations, the rocket sailplane was carried to an altitude of 36000 feet on the back of a Dornier 217K.

When it was released it could reach a height of 76000 feet and when it crossed its target, it used two fuselage-mounted Zeiss infrared cameras. Astonishingly, at this time in the war, it could maintain its reconnaissance altitude for forty five minutes and glide down to 40000 feet in 465 miles. These altitudes could be substantially increased by using upward rising air currents. A development of the D.F.S.228 was the supersonic D.F.S.346, which was expected to reach an altitude of 66000 feet, after leaving the parent aircraft at 33000 feet. The development of the D.F.S.346 was undertaken by Junkers. In their design series it became the Junkers S/8-346. Heinkel was given sub-contract work by Messerschmitt on developments of their rocket fighters, but none of the Heinkel fighters entered service by the war's end.

In the field of sonic research, it was left to the firm of Junkers to develop the concept of the hypersonic aircraft. Due to Allied bombing, many of the aircraft companies, including Junkers, set up assembly facilities underground. At Tarthum, a huge salt mine was dug out by slave labour for the Junkers Company who, by 1945, had developed the S-346 all metal reconnaissance aeroplanes further. Following the, by now, German practice of utilising all the available powerplants which were then in production, the Junkers S-346 was powered by the same engine as the Me163 and the D.F.S.228, the Walter 109-509a liquid-fuelled rocket engine. The wing had a forty five degree sweep, with an area of 216 square feet and a span of 30 feet. Initially designed to have a single rocket motor, it was felt that the metal fuselage could quite easily accommodate two Walter rocket motors and these were successfully installed. Underneath the fuselage was a retractable landing skid and in the nose was the pilot's pressure cabin. The whole nose could be blown off by means of explosive bolts and a parachute was used to slow its descent. Due to the pioneering nature of the work, the Junkers Company was advised by the Aerodynamische Versuchsanstalt (Aerodynamic Research Institute) of Gottingen. They worked out the flutter velocities of the S-346 over a whole range of Mach numbers and helped with the initial design details. The first gliding flight was planned not to exceed 560 mph and after it landed, all the test data would be correlated and the design modified accordingly. In addition to Junkers manufacturing the type, at least three others were manufactured by Siebel on sub-contract work. The Junkers S-346 was a highly ambitious and practical supersonic aeroplane. At altitude, the Junkers S-346 could quite easily have attained 1250 mph and climbing vertically was clearly possible. But what struck the Allied inspection team was the shape of the fuselage, which was almost identical to that of the Lockheed P-80 Shooting Star, which was just about to enter USAAF service. When the war ended, the salt mine at Tarthum was cleared by the Allies and on the 27th June 1945, the Junkers S-346, supersonic, research aeroplane, was crated by the Allies and sent to England. As for the Siebel examples, they were captured by Soviet forces and sent to Russia. D.F.S.228, D-IBFQ came to England in August 1945, but was not displayed at the German aircraft trophy exhibition at Farnborough. It was sent to Slingsby Sailplanes, where it was rebuilt. Painted a high gloss cream overall, the D.F.S.228 was returned to Farnborough. Its fate is obscure, but it was possibly sent to the United States, to join the Junkers S-346, for further trials.

There had been a strong suspicion at the Air Ministry that the D.F.S. series of rocket sailplanes had been partly operational. One or two officers believed that the reconnaissance photographs which the Germans had obtained of the Normandy beachhead and of the Allied advance into the Low Countries, in the summer of 1944, had been carried out by the D.F.S.228. But in retrospect, the laurels went to Arado.

In the Soviet Union, tests started with the D.F.S.346. In 1947, it was mounted under the wing of a North American Mitchell and in September 1948 it was dropped from a Soviet TU-4, a copy of the B-29, but as a result of a heavy landing, the pilot was injured and the airframe damaged. In 1951, a third example was built, but it broke up in the air, the carrier aircraft being once again a TU-4. The pilot escaped by deploying the escape capsule. The aircraft managed to reach Mach 0.9 on one occasion and 590 mph on another. As a result of continual failure of the test programme, the Soviets abandoned the research programme.

The D.F.S.228 and a Dornier Mother Plane

D.F.S.228 in flight and preparing to land

Impression of the D.F.S.346

Miles

The development of the rocket plane in Britain took a decidedly back seat, due to the progress of the gas turbine at Frank Whittle's Power Jets. By 1941, Power Jets had succeeded in producing the first British jet aircraft, in collaboration with the Gloster Aircraft Company and were on the verge of having their designs mass-produced by a variety of manufacturers. The existence of the supersonic intelligence report and its circulation among the leading British airframe manufacturers, brought an interest in supersonic aircraft from an unusual source.

The aircraft manufacturing firm of Miles had entered the aeroplane field before the war as Phillips & Powis, with Rolls-Royce as the major shareholder. With vast stocks of Rolls-Royce Kestrel aero engines being available and many being reconditioned, this powerplant was installed in the Phillips & Powis Miles Master 1 fighter-trainer. As an emergency fighter, Miles also produced the all-wood, bubble-canopied M.20, single seat fighter, powered by the Rolls-Royce Merlin, which was in "power-egg" form, as adopted for the Merlin-engined Beaufighter. Though this fighter had comparable performance to the early Hurricane, Spitfire and Defiant, it did not go into production. By 1943, the firm of Miles had produced a variety of wooden training aircraft for the Royal Air Force and these included the Master and the Magister.

F.G.Miles had already broken new ground with his own revolutionary design of a tandem-wing aeroplane, the Miles Libellula. Much of the theoretical work of this wooden aircraft was undertaken in Glasgow. Though the Libellula had not been ordered by the Air Ministry, Miles still had the capacity to produce unusual aeroplanes. During 1943, Miles was approached by Rolls-Royce to produce a single-engined research fighter, to be built around their new piston engine, the Rolls-Royce Griffon. Much of this aeroplane design was influenced by the North American Mustang, but it departed from convention, by having its powerplant buried inside the rear fuselage. Two factors influenced Miles in dropping the Rolls-Royce Griffon fighter; firstly, the circulation of the Air Ministry's report on German supersonic fighters and secondly, the development of the gas turbine for aircraft.

Power Jets had developed a whole series of engines which were finally entering service in the Gloster Meteor as Rolls-Royce powerplants. Frank Whittle had gone on to produce the Power Jets three-stage W.2/700, which was designed for supersonic flight. It was also Whittle's last design to go into an aircraft. The Miles Company saw that merging the W.2/700 with an airframe would give Britain an aeroplane with supersonic capabilities and advance the science of aero engines and airframes further. Miles proposed a new aircraft, designated the M.52, to an Air Ministry specification E.24/43. It was to be a single seat, supersonic aircraft, built from light alloy, with a semi-monocoque fuselage and be able to fly at over 1000 mph. The M.52 evolved under the leadership of F.G.Miles, L.C.Heal, H.S. Wilkinson and D.S.Bancroft.

Initially designed to fly subsonically on the first stage of the W.2/700, the M.52 would then fly transonically, powered by the ducted fan of the engine's second stage. It would then fly supersonically, using the thrust of the final afterburner, taking the M.52 through the sound barrier, into supersonic flight. The Ministry of Aircraft Production granted Miles funds for pursuing the design and many wooden models were built to support the project. The M.52 aerofoil sections were truly knife-edged and razor thin in the trailing and leading edge sections. All the tail surfaces were made moveable. The pilot's cockpit was set in the nose, which was designed to blow off with explosive bolts. A parachute was installed in the rear of the nose cabin wall to slow the descent. The pilot would then bale out and use his own parachute.

To test the design of the wings and tailplane of the M.52, a full set of wooden aerofoil surfaces were fitted to a pre-war Miles M3B Falcon Six (L9705). Delivered to the Royal Aircraft Establishment at Farnborough in 1937, L9705 tested a variety of aerofoil wing sections, including Clark and NACA designs. During trials, one wing would have pointed tips, while the other would have its roots built up or, on other trials, the wings would have blunt tips or both wing roots built up in an aerofoil section. As such, L9705 was ideal for the test

Miles M.52 mock-up in wood

Impressions of the M.52 in flight

Miles "Gillette" Falcon, used to test the M.52 aerofoil surfaces

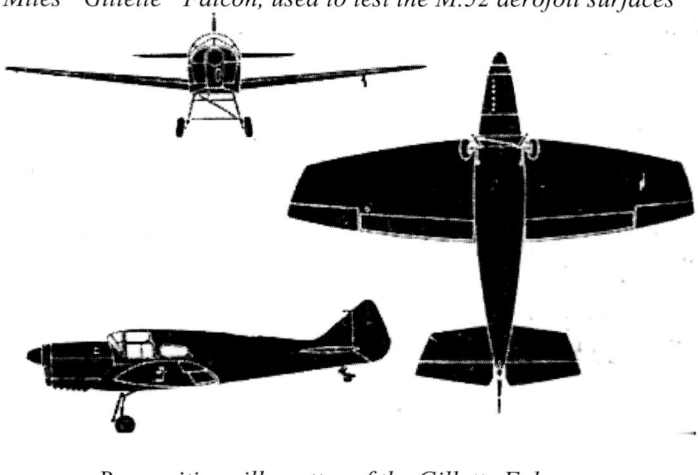

Recognition silhouettes of the Gillette Falcon with M.52 flying surfaces

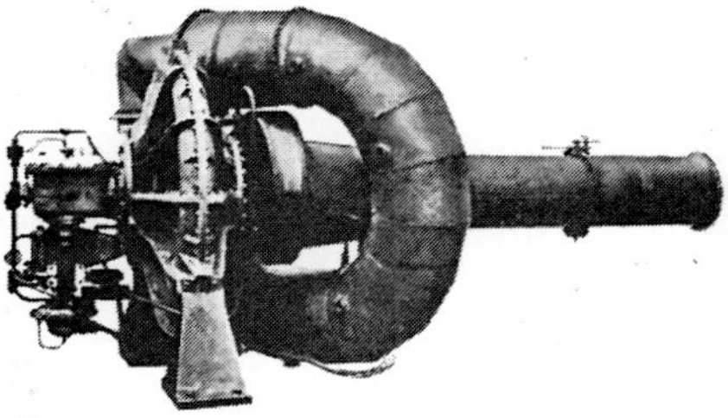

The first Whittle gas-turbine engine.

Early Whittle jet engines

Power Jets W.2/700, designed for the Miles M.52

Power Jets W.2/700 fitted to the tail of a test Wellington

work for the M.52 project and in 1944, it was delivered to the Miles factory at Woodley for conversion. At Farnborough, the Falcon was joined by Bell Kingcobra, FZ440, which commenced tests in a similar role. The Falcon L9705 had its undercarriage replaced with a Miles M.38 Messenger unit, the wings were modified with knife-edged leading and trailing surfaces and later, the tail of the M.52 was fitted. L9705 was made a single-seater by the addition of extra fuel tanks in the cockpit and the installation of test instrumentation. Now christened the "Gillette Falcon", the converted M.3B first flew at Woodley on 11th August 1944, but for its first flight it had the normal Falcon tail surfaces. In later test flights, the Falcon had the M.52 tailplane fitted, but with separate elevators. Later it was refitted with the all-flying tailplane of the original M.52 design. This was the first aeroplane to be designed from the outset with an all-flying tail. By all accounts, the conversion work on the M.3B was successful, but a measure of doubt began to creep into the whole supersonic project.

During the spring of 1945, a succession of trials was carried out with rocket models which had had their tail surfaces replaced by scale units from the M.52. Other tests were carried out on a high speed rail track, with M.52 models and more models had been dropped from high altitude to test the flight envelope of the soon to be completed full-scale aircraft. Wind tunnel tests were also carried out, but the culmination of all these tests was to be a disaster for Miles. It was discovered that the M.52 became unstable about the longitudinal axis as it reached high Mach numbers and that this instability continued as it passed through the sound barrier. There was the added problem of landing the M.52 at 170 mph, with a run of two miles and the virtual impossibility of the pilot escaping from the aircraft if anything happened.

Now came a further problem - the survival of the Power Jets W.2/700. Though the government had nationalised Power Jets in 1944 and many of Power Jets designs were taken over by Rolls-Royce, the future of the W.2/700 was uncertain. As an aircraft powerplant, it was derived from the W.2/500, which when taken over by Rolls-Royce, became the Derwent and went on to power the Gloster Meteor. As a new gas turbine, just on the verge of being cleared from prototype to production, the W.2/700 had no place in the

Rolls-Royce aero-engine field and although it had flown in a Gloster Meteor and the E28/39, it disappeared into obscurity.(Some examples were built in the United states by the General Electric Company as the I-16) When all these factors were taken into account by the Ministry of Aircraft Production and finally the Air Ministry, it was quite clear that the Miles M.52 project was not a viable proposition and early in 1946 the Miles M.52 was cancelled. This decision denied Britain the laurels of being first to break the sound barrier. The prize went to Bell in the United States, in 1947.

Gloster E28/39 W4041, used for W.2/700 high speed trials, August 1944. Tests were made up to a Mach number of 0·72 when a longitudinal pitching oscillation of the aircraft developed

Rolls-Royce Derwent-powered Gloster Meteors

Butterfly and Enzian

During the Second World War, Germany had produced a succession of ground to air and air to ground missiles, powered by liquid rocket and powder motors for anti-aircraft use. It was only in 1932 that Germany first raised a specification for a "Barrage Fire Rocket", but nothing was done on this project until 1939. The Luftwaffe had established "C Office" for the procurement and supply of materiel for the air force. A branch, headed by Chief Technologist Lt. Bree, was formed within this office for the development of rocket technology. At the beginning of 1941, Branch 6 of the Luftwaffe drew up a specification for a remotely controlled anti-aircraft rocket. The project came under the control of the Austrian, Major Friedrich Halder, who had studied rocketry at university and who was on the staff of Branch 6. He was assisted by Lieutenant Stoezel, who was an army field officer. Stoezel had enthusiastically put forward ideas on anti-aircraft rocketry that, so much so, he was transferred to Peenemunde under Dornberger and von Braun. The project was interrupted by an edict from Hitler on 11th September 1941, cancelling all long term development projects.

Under the cover of small experimental work, Stoezel continued his researches. He obtained two tank chassis and converted one for rocket use, by fitting twelve rocket barrels onto the chassis. There was no sight or tracking device on the tank to engage an aircraft. This weakness came to light, when the tank was sent to the Russian front in 1943. The test was a failure. This failure was also caused by lack of direction on policy; neither the Luftwaffe nor the Army would take authority for the project.

Earlier, on 1st September 1942, Goering had signed an order for procurement and development of rockets for an anti-aircraft programme. By the spring of 1943, a separate department was established at Peenemunde for anti-aircraft rocket research, coming under the command of Major Halder. Though Halder had the experience, he was only given around 200 men to get the project going. Few had the technical experience to carry through the project and the manpower size fluctuated with the demands of other departments and the war. With only 160 men at any one time, Halder calculated that it would be between two and three years before they could provide any rockets for anti-aircraft work. The project was hampered by inter-service rivalry for raw materials and the interference of high officials who had influence on Hitler. For example, Speer had persuaded Hitler that gas launchers could be used to fire rockets at aircraft, in barrages. Hitler agreed and with the agreement came a change in policy. There was also the problem of providing accurate electronics for guidance systems. For a time, the project verged on cancellation, but it was realised that the Luftwaffe could not cope with Allied escort fighters and bombers and the project was revived. Another edict from Hitler ordered that a 210mm smoke launcher be utilised for AA defence. This device was to be used in the defence of the Ruhr. It was felt that, by keeping the launchers close together, they would be able to create a fire barrier.

With the increase in bomber activities and the threat it imposed on the Reich, a new branch was formed, to take over all research and development activities for rockets. This was known as Branch E (AAA). C-Office raised no objection to this. Halder was now given responsibility for all anti-aircraft rocket development.

Anti-aircraft Artillery came under the auspices of three offices, the Army, the Air Force and Albert Speer's Munitions Ministry. It was only under Major Halder that any development was allowed to continue. Halder became the subject of inter-service and inter-ministry rivalry, but by using his authority, he managed to keep the rocket projects going. Halder secured the support of the research station at Peenemunde and was able to obtain the results of experimental rocket work done there. He also established a research station near Peenemunde, but its construction was hampered by the Air Force, which was to supply the building materials. It was only by the middle of 1943 that things started to progress.

The first rocket to be designed had a range of 24 miles and an altitude of 52800 feet. It had a proximity fuse and remote control from a ground station. These powder rockets went into production at Rheinmetall and the Bruenner armament works in December 1942.

Early German rocket researchers, Oberth standing to the right of the rocket, Von Braun second from the right

Peenemunde rocket team, Dornberger third from the left, von Braun fourth from the left

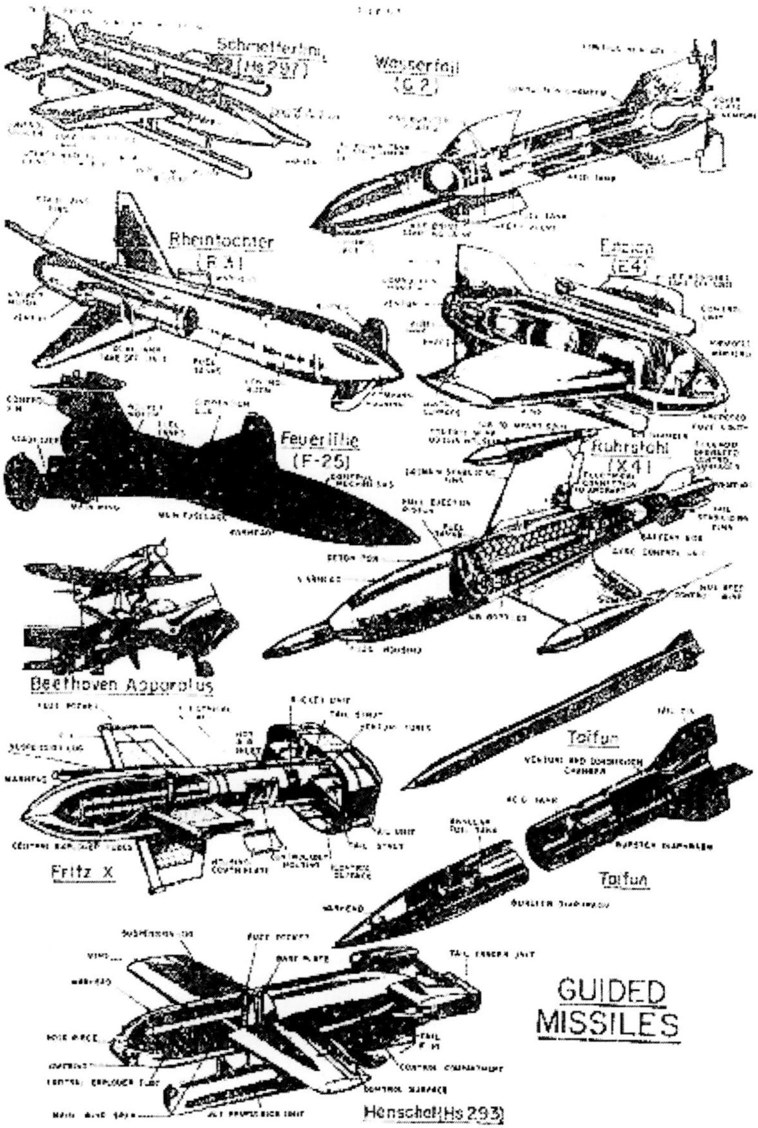

Allied technical handbook illustrating German guided missiles

Fohn rocket launcher

"Orkan" under the wings of a prototype 163

Later, in October 1943, trials were conducted with the "Fohn" rocket launcher. This launcher was mounted on a trailer with 35 rocket tubes and had a calibre of 73mm. The warhead weighed 2.2 pounds and with a speed of 400ft per second, it had a range of just under one mile. 50 were produced in 1942 and by 1945, 85 were still in service, providing cover for river crossings. Another powder rocket, the 50/55 mm R4M "Orkan" was tested, but never went into production for anti-aircraft service. Orkan did achieve some success as a converted, air-launched, anti-aircraft missile with the Me262. Air tests had also been carried out by an Me110 and an Me163. R4Ms also had the same ballistic characteristics as the MK 108 cannon, which meant that the Me262 could use the same sight for both weapons.

The next rocket was the "Taifun", which was being developed under Ing. Wilhelm Burkhardt. It measured less than 100mm in diameter and 190 centimetres in length, Taifun weighed around 30 pounds and carried a 1.4-pound warhead. The Germans fired the rockets in ripples, from either a 30-barrel or 50-barrel launcher, mounted on an 88 mm gun carriage. The Taifun had an altitude capability of 46000 to 52000 feet. Designs were submitted to the Hoichsluftfahrt Ministerium in September 1944 and accepted and frozen in October. Scheufelen was made the "Sachbearbeiter", or administrative officer, in charge of development at Peenemunde. Actual production of finished rounds began in January 1945 and it is certain that over 600 out of the first projected batch of 10000 were completed before the German surrender. In January 1945, plans had

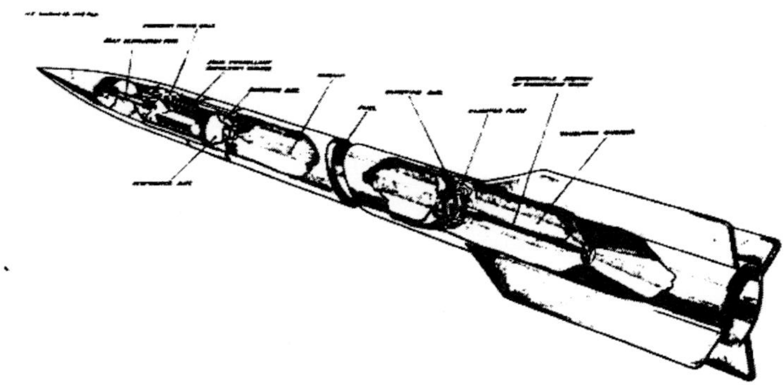

TAIFUN

LIQUID FUELLED ANTI-AIRCRAFT ROCKET

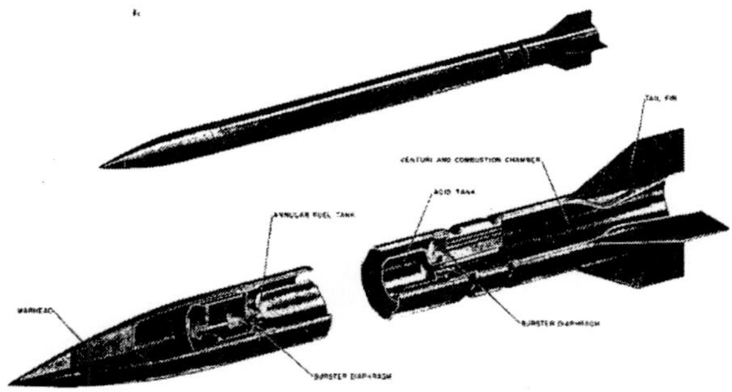

Figure 199—Taifun

Allied technical breakdown of Taifun

been made for the creation of 400 Taifun batteries, which would be in service by October 1945. In addition to the solid-fuelled Taifun there was a liquid-fuelled version, Taifun F. The liquid-fuelled Taifun F had advantages over the solid rocket version. These are indicated below: -

(a) Due to the special design of combustion chamber, which gives an almost instantaneous rise of thrust from zero to its full value, the velocity and speed of rotation on leaving the projector were relatively high. This minimises the usually considerable errors at this point of its flight, when the fins have little effect.

(b) In solid-fuelled rockets, just before the final burn, pieces of unburnt propellant were liable to be thrown out as the remaining propellant broke up. This caused dispersion, as was apparently evident in a series of flight photographs, taken by Burkhurdt, of the solid-fuelled Taifun. No such dispersion was evident in similar photographs of the liquid-fuelled version of the rocket.

(c) There was no dispersion due to the heating up and consequent distortion of the fuselage of the rocket,

(d) The exhaust gas flow was more uniform over its cross-section, giving a more accurate axial thrust.

The Germans had high hopes for Taifun and had projected five versions:-

Taifun F. (German notation)

This was the model in quantity production at the end of the war, having a 10cm. outer diameter and 2.5 second burning time.

Taifun 1. (British numbering)

This was similar model using higher expulsion and combustion pressures and the same venturi, giving a shorter burning time of 1.5 seconds. This model reached the stage of static tests.

Taifun 2.

This model was the same as the two previously mentioned, in size and weight, working at higher pressures, but with a different injector and venturi. This had a still shorter burning time of 0.8 to 1.0 seconds and had reached the stage of flight trials.

Taifun 3.

This was a projected design for a 7cm model, of lighter weight and the same performance as the previous models, when carrying the same warhead. It was considered to be the most economical design to give this performance,

Taifun 4.

This was a smaller, 5cm model for shorter range work, with the same warhead.

The General Staff felt Taifun was far too large and uneconomical. It also lacked a homing device, which was essential for its use and much trouble was experienced in the initial firings.

Intelligence Report

Taifun was a bi-liquid rocket, designed to be fired in groups of 65 from a launching machine known as the "Dobgerate". From all indications, it never passed beyond the experimental stage.

The projectile is approximately 2.1metres long and 10centimetres in diameter. The greater part is taken up with the fuel tanks, which contain Visol and acid. The acid is housed in a central, aluminium tank, while the Visol is contained in the annular tank between the inside tank and the outer skin of the missile. The walls of both tanks are 1 mm thick. The acid tank is supported in the rocket shell by two aluminium end-plates, bolted to its end flanges. These end plates are perforated, so as to connect the fuel tanks at the upper end to the cartridge pot and at the lower end, to the liquid sprays. A thin, aluminium rupturing diaphragm covers the holes in the two end plates.

Behind the solid steel nose-piece, there is a hollow chamber for housing the 500 grams of explosive, the impact fuse and the igniting device for setting off the cartridge pot. The cartridge pot is just aft of the chamber which houses the warhead and the fusing system. When the contents of the cartridge pot begin to burn, a gas is generated which is used to expel the liquids from the tanks and force them into the combustion chamber. The combustion chamber and venturi are made of mild steel, mostly 1mm thick, but the thickness increases at the venturi throat to 2.5 to 3mm. At the end of 2 seconds operation, the temperature of the venturi reached 300°C to 400°C. It was possible to use a venturi experimentally for five runs, after which it had to be renewed.

TECHNICAL DATA:

Dimensions
Total length: 2.10metres.
Maximum diameter: 0.10 metre.

Length of tanks:
Acid tank: 1.15metres.
Annular tank: 1.20metres.
Diameter of tanks:
Acid tank: 0.08metre.
Annular tank: 0.10metre.

Weights:
Nose Piece; 1.30kg.
Outer Shell: 3.25kg.
Tanks; 1.75kg.
Combustion Chamber: 1.50kg.
Thrust Block: 0.73kg.
Thrust Disk: 0.70kg.
Rest: 1.77kg.
Total (empty): 11.00kg.
Charge in Warhead: 0.50kg.
Expellant Cartridge: 0.50kg.
Acid: 8.60 kg,
Fuel (Visol): 2.30kg.
Total (loaded):22.90kg

The development of Taifun was closely linked with another anti-aircraft rocket, "Wasserfall". There is evidence to suggest that the same fuels were initially developed for both Wasserfall and Taifun and incorporating the new method of fuel expulsion, using gas produced by burning cordite.

Wasserfall takes to the air

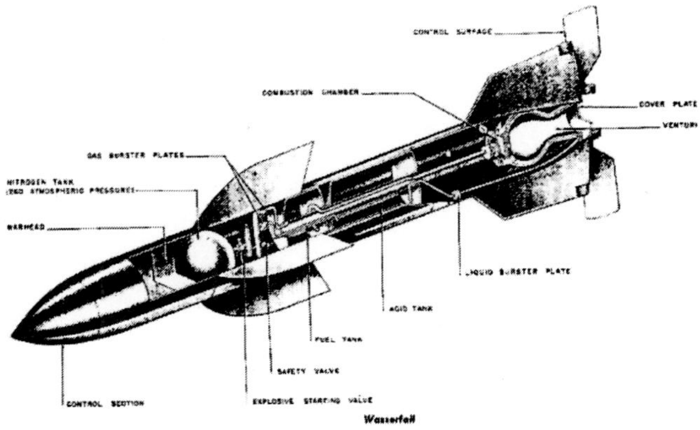

Allied technical inspection drawing of Wasserfall

It is not clear whether this was a development of attempts to use cordite expulsion for Wasserfall, or whether this method was being tried out for Taifun and Wasserfall simultaneously. It is known, however, that while little success was achieved with the longer burning times of the larger projectile, probably owing to the burning-out of pipes etc., satisfactory firings were obtained with the shorter burning times of Typhoon. It seems probable that this followed tests of Typhoon, fitted with the motor of the later Wasserfall.

Wasserfall, or C-2, was a promising rocket, resembling a junior V2. A supersonic missile, it was designed to destroy an aircraft flying at 560 miles per hour at 65,000 feet, at a horizontal range of 30 miles. It measured 25 feet long and weighed 4 tons on the ground. Launched vertically, like the V2, it generated about a 9 ton thrust for about 45 seconds. In that time, it accelerated to a speed of 2,500 feet per second (1700 miles per hour and almost the 2,805 feet per second speed of an Ml rifle bullet). This speed was achieved upon attaining an altitude of 60000 feet. Initially, the German guidance system was to provide two radar sets for tracking, with radio for control. Later, an infrared proximity fuse and homing device were scheduled for installation.

Though the design was finished in 1943 and 25 missiles had been fired and final operational tests completed in January of 1945, the

Wasserfall development was not concluded before the war's end. The Germans had nevertheless begun work on its production, hoping that it would be the high altitude flak weapon that they needed so badly.

Intelligence Report

This flak rocket was given the name Wasserfall and the designation C-2 8/45. The C-2 was designed to be launched vertically from the ground, travelling at supersonic speed, to be guided into bomber formations, where it would be exploded. The Wasserfall resembled a half-size V2 with small wings. It had a similar motor and was launched in much the same manner. Its control gear was also similar. It could reach a maximum speed of about 770 metres per second in about 45 seconds, after which time the speed would decrease as the fuel was exhausted. It could still chase targets until its speed had dropped to about 350 metres per second. Its maximum fighting ranges were: 18 kilometres in height and 26 kilometres in horizontal range. It was designed to withstand manoeuvres of up to 4.4g. The missile was guided by radio signals from the ground, until approaching the target, at which time a self-contained homing system was to lead it in. It was planned to incorporate a proximity fuse to explode the weapon close to the bombers. With these properties, the Germans expected every other missile to bring down a bomber making 2g evasive manoeuvres at a speed of 250 metres per second.

OPERATIONAL ASPECTS

A. The Wasserfall was planned for use from the ground against air targets, specifically bombers. Suggested locations for launching sites were along the French coast and the approaches to major targets of bombers.

B. The launching site required much equipment and although mobile, would thus be subject to attack. Lack of manoeuvrability against relatively slow airplanes would have inhibited its effectiveness.

C. The Wasserfall was expected to be both cheaper and more effective than ordinary flak for the results obtained. Only operational use could prove this point.

Conclusions: The Wasserfall was not completed and thus offers no immediate possibilities as a weapon, without much further work on the control system.

RECOMMENDATIONS. It is believed that an intensive study of the Wasserfall will yield much information on the principles and the use of a supersonic guided missile.

A. AIRFRAME. TYPE AND DESCRIPTION. In overall appearance the Wasserfall resembles a half-size V-2 with small wings. The approximate dimensions are:-

Length: 7800mm. Calibre: 880mm. Wing span: 1890mm. Tail span: 2500mm.

There were four small, biconvex dorsal wings at the centre of gravity, to assist in making turns. In line with these wings were four stabilizing fins at the tail. Control surfaces were fitted on the stabilizing fins, both in the air stream and in the gas stream of the jet motor.

B. AERODYNAMIC CHARACTERISITICS. The Wasserfall was designed to catch, while travelling at supersonic speed, a target having a velocity of 250 metres per second, doing 2g manoeuvres. Essentially the missile travels at and was designed for supersonic speeds. However, the transition from zero speed at launching, to the supersonic range, was not instantaneous and some additional control was desirable during this interval. This was supplied by the gas stream fins, which are present for the first 5-15 seconds of flight. Once the supersonic range was reached, the air stream fins supply sufficient control, while the jet stream fins add drag. Consequently, they are jettisoned at that time. The missile was designed to stand manoeuvres up to 4.4g. The wings supported a lift of 8000kg per pair, to which the body, tail, etc., add about another 4000kg making a total lift of 12000kg. The missile weighs about 3500kg at take-off, but the weight drops continually to about 1500kg by the time the fuel is exhausted. Thus, at take-off, the lateral acceleration did not exceed 3g, increasing to 4.4g as the fuel was consumed. To allow for this, the control applied to the servo is made weak at first and is gradually brought up to its full power. Wind tunnel tests of models may be found in report No.UM6013, dated February 1945, in the Gottingen documents. Evidence obtained at the wind tunnels at Kochel shows that at least six different shapes had been tried out to get the best aerodynamic results.

C. DESIGN DATA. The missile was fabricated from mild steel. It may be broken down into the following parts:-

1. Nose: Contains the homing device (zielsuchendes Geraet) fuses (Zuender) and explosive (Sprengstoff).
2. Nitrogen tank: (Druckluftbehaelter).
3. Visol tank: (Brennstoffhaelter).
4. Wings: (Fluogel).
5. Salbei tank: (Salbeibehaelter).
6. Control system: Mounted to rear of Salbei Tank.
7. Tail: Supports motor (Brennkammer), tails (Flosse), air rudders (Luftruder) and jet rudders (Stahlrader).

D. PRODUCTION DATA. The following remarks apply to all parts of the missile. The only production was by the Electromechanische Werke at Peenemunde, for developmental testing. Estimates of production range from 40 to 275 units. Estimates were drawn up for the men, material and space needed for the mass production of 5000 per month.

A. PROPULSION SYSTEM. Type and Description.

A liquid jet motor drive is used, which develops an 8,000 kg thrust for 45 seconds. The motor burns a self-igniting mixture of Salbei (nitric acid) and Visol (a hydro-carbon mixture) in a chamber with a venturi nozzle.

B. CHARACTERISTICS.

Thrust: 8000kg. Total impulse: 360000kg. Launching acceleration: 1.2 to 2.6g. Final acceleration: Ca. 4g. Fuel consumption: 41 kg/sec. Specific impulse: 180 to 195sec.

C. DESIGN DATA. The foremost flask contains nitrogen at a pressure of 200-300atmos. This flask was 8 to 13mm thick and was not wire wound. The compressed gas passes through a reducing valve to 30atmos and was used to force the liquids out of their storage tanks. This flask and the two storage tanks were made of rolled and welded steel. The forward storage tank contains about 400kg or 430 litres of Visol. Visol was a rather variable fuel, according to the ingredients available, or the intended use. A typical Visol mixture was: 40 percent isopropyl alcohol; 40 percent vinyl ether; 2 percent water; 18 percent of four other ingredients, including 1 percent dope, to control the ignition delay time. Visol was a contracted code name for vinylisobutylether. Diesel oil may also be used in place of Visol. The rear tank contained about 1500kg or 1100litres of the oxidant Salbei. Salbei was a mixture of 90 percent nitric acid (including 3 percent water) and 10 percent sulphuric acid. No attempt was made to make the acid water-free, as it would be reabsorbed from the air before it was ever used. The sulphuric acid was added to prevent corrosion by the nitric acid of the steel available for the tanks. As was already mentioned, the fuel and oxidant were forced out by pressure. The fuel was removed through a swinging pipe hanging down in the tanks. As this pipe was subjected to the same acceleration as the fuel, its end was always covered by liquid. This design gave a lightweight removal system, which removed practically the last drop of liquid, although the liquids were being swished around in the tanks. It was said that this system increased the maximum altitude obtainable by 4 kilo-metres over a pump arrangement that was tried. Both fuel and oxidant were passed through a valving arrangement, which introduced both liquids into the motor at the same time under full flow. Valves in the various pipe lines were opened simultaneously by explosive charges. Just before each liquid entered the motor, was a diaphragm. These diaphragms stopped the liquid until it had built up to practically full pressure, at which time the diaphragm burst and allowed a full flow of liquid to enter the motor. The ratio of liquids by weight is Salbei to Visol from 5 to 1 up to 8 to 1, depending upon the actual Visol mixture being used. The Visol was fed directly to the nozzle head. The Salbei first passed through the cooling jacket of the motor, before going to the nozzle head. In some cases, some of the Salbei is also injected through cooling holes into the combustion chamber. The two liquids ignite within 0.01 to 0.1 second after contact. An expansion ratio of 2.5 to 1 up to 3.9 to 1 was obtained in the motor. The gas exit velocity is approximately 1850 metres per second. Brennschluss (turning off of the motor) had not been settled. Provisions were made for several methods, which were:-

1. Letting the motor use up all of the fuel
2. Turning off the motor by radio signal
3. Turning off the motor at a predetermined velocity by means of an integrating accelerometer.

Of the other principal flak missiles, the Rheintochter went through several versions. It was a development of Hermann Goering's great Rheinmetall-Borsig arms firm. The Rheintochter I was fired from an altered 88mm Flak carriage. Tests were initially conducted with models at Laba on the Baltic coast, which were very successful. The trials included tests with unguided starts, at an angle of 60 degrees, with pre-determined programming using sub and supersonic missiles. The rudder was set at an angle of 6 degrees, with small resistance strips attached to two opposite vanes, producing a rolling motion. The tests took place between April and November 1943.

Rheintochter I was a subsonic, solid-fuel, two-stage rocket that measured 20.5 feet and weighed 3,850 pounds. The second stage had four canard fins and six wings (which spanned 9.8 feet) and carried a 330-pound warhead to a slant range of 18000 yards and an altitude of 29000 feet. The Germans first tested the radio-controlled device in August 1943 and fired 82 flak rockets by early January 1945.The Germans cancelled the program the next month. Rheintochter II employed two booster rockets, as did Rheintochter III. The third version used the same first stage, but its second stage was about 3.3 feet longer. It was powered by a liquid-fuel engine and had slightly better performance than its predecessor, having the ability to reach an altitude of almost 50000 feet at a range of over 20,000 yards. The Germans tested about six of these (none with radio control), between July 1944 and January 1945, before cancelling Rheintochter in favour of the Schmetterling. Even with its cancellation, Rheinmetall continued research and development work. In a series of successful tests, Rheinmetall proved the concept of the weapon and its guidance system, which was of optical sighting. This was a very important step forward and the outcome was that work was allowed to continue on the Rheintochter project. It was only with the collapse of Germany in 1945 that the Rheintochter project stopped.

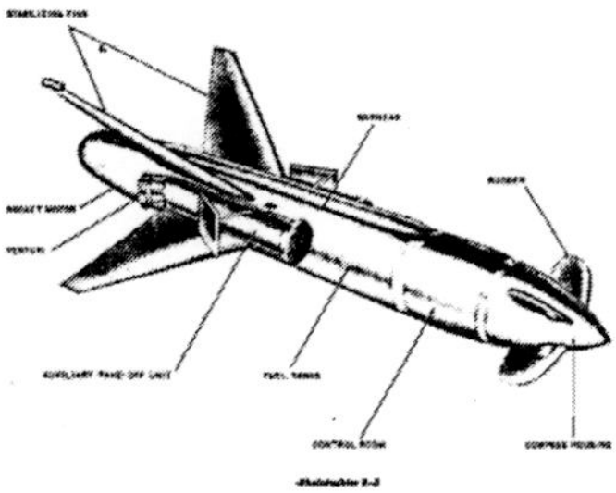

Rheintochter

Schmetterling was developed by the firm of Hansche Flugzeugwerke at Berlin-Schönefeld as the Hs177 (Hs297). It had a length of 4metres and a diameter of 280mm. It had arrow-like wings and ailerons of 35cm in length and a wing span of 2.8metres. Its overall weight was 450 kilogrammes. It had an explosive charge of 40 kilogrammes. Each starter rocket weighed 85 kilogrammes and contained 40 kilogrammes of Diglycol powder. The starter rockets had a thrust of 1750 kilogrammes and burned for about four seconds. The rockets were set at an angle of 30 degrees. After discarding its

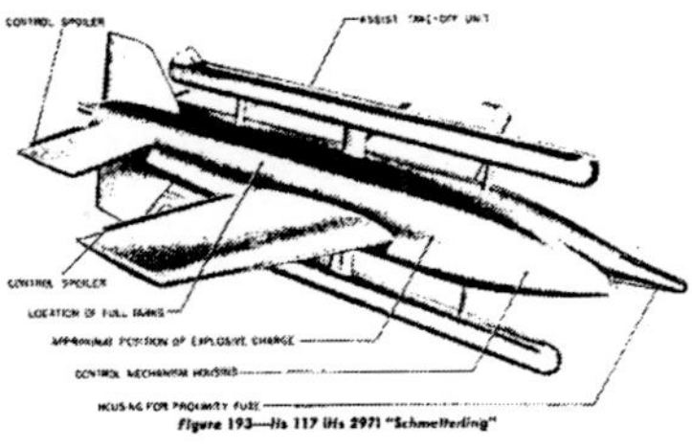

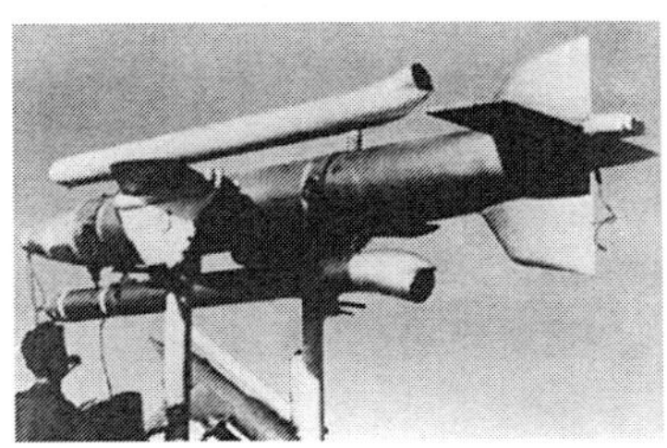

Schmetterling

powder rockets, it still had a weight of 270 kilogrammes. The fuselage and wings were of light metal construction. It was controlled by a gunner, who would guide the missile to the target for about 2 kilometres, to about 7 metres from the target. The round was fired by a proximity fuse. The first designs were submitted in July 1943. In some of its early trials, misses of about 25 metres were recorded and, by January 1944, the first trial models were completed. The trials were delayed when the test rockets were destroyed in an air raid. The AAA Department felt that Schmetterling was the most economical AA missile to produce. The decision to produce AA missiles was in the hands of Goering and in October 1944, he made his decision. To the consternation of the General Staff, Goering chose Enzian, which had not even reached the development stage. Schmetterling had been the recommended choice

Intelligence Report Hs177 Schmetterling

DESCRIPTION: This missile, probably better known as the "Schmetterling", was a rocket propelled, radio-controlled missile for use against bomber formations. Some versions were for ground-to-air and some for air-to-air operations. The fuselage was of the conventional type, with a single vertical tail surface and a single horizontal surface. The horizontal surface was mounted well above the centre line of the fuselage. The arrowhead wing was mounted on the centre line of the fuselage. The forward section of the fuselage was asymmetrical, in order to accommodate a proximity fuse and a propeller-driven generator. This missile was launched from the ground from a simple, two-armed, zero-length rail launcher. The two arms supported the missile at the wing roots at about the centre of gravity. Two assisted take-off units were used for ground launching, one above and one below the fuselage. At the end of burning, these ATO units were jettisoned by means of explosive bolts, which threw them clear from the airframe. The air-launched version did not use ATO units, but was simply dropped from a standard bomb shackle. Some of these models were automatically homed and some were remotely controlled. A single gyro automatic pilot was used for stabilization.

DETAILS

AIRFRAME TYPE AND DESCRIPTION

Model C. The main units of the fuel system formed the backbone of the fuselage. At the forward end was the steel air flask, nested into the forward end of an aluminium Salbei tank. Next came an aluminium casting, through which passed the main wing spar and which was also used to space the hydrocarbon tank further aft, for the proper distribution of the c.g. of the fuel, since it was desired to have the fuel c.g. coincide with the c.g. of the entire aircraft. On the after end of the hydrocarbon tank another aluminium casting was bolted, which supported the main propulsion unit and the air stabilizer structure. All of these tanks and castings were securely bolted together, forming the entire backbone of the aircraft. This structure was covered with sheet aluminium. The nose section, also formed of aluminium, was screwed to the forward end. The wing and tail were built-up sections, consisting of a cast magnesium frame, with an aluminium covering. The cast magnesium wing frame was extremely light in weight and was rigid.

AERODYNAMIC CHARACTERISTICS

This missile was controlled in roll by spoilers on the trailing edges of the wings. These spoilers work out of phase with one another. The missile was controlled in elevation by trailing edge spoilers on the horizontal stabilizer. These spoilers work in phase with one another. Yaw was controlled by the trailing edge spoilers on the wings. Spoiler control was used for this model, because, as in other missiles, it gave adequate and easy control, as compared to other systems and produced less drag. The spoilers also present a much more simple method of control than other systems. This missile was rather unique in that assisted take-off rockets were placed, both above and below the fuselage, mounted in the vertical plane of the centre line of the fuselage. It was also interesting to note the extent of asymmetry of the forward portion of the fuselage. It was considered by the designer, Prof. Wagner, that horizontal asymmetry would be less harmful than vertical asymmetry, the asymmetry being necessary to correctly place the generator propeller and the fuse. For reasons of stability, the missile, upon ground launching, made at least one complete roll about its longitudinal axis. If, at the end of this roll, the air speed is not great enough for adequate stability, it would make a second complete roll. Seldom, however, was the second roll necessary. This roll event is built into the control equipment and is entirely automatic.

DESIGN AND PERFORMANCE DATA: PRINCIPAL DIMENSIONS

Length overall: 429cm.
Length of fuselage: 369cm.
Span of wings: 200cm.
Height of vertical rudder: 92 cm
Diameter of fuselage: 35cm.

PRINCIPAL WEIGHTS

Weight empty: 150kg.
Launching weight: 430kg.
Weight at target: 175kg.
Weight of assisted take-off units: (each 90Kg) 180kg.
Main power oxidizer: 59.2kg.
Compressed air: 3kg.
Explosive: 25kg.

PERFORMANCE

Maximum velocity: 250m/sec.
Average velocity: 240m/sec.
Maximum range: 20km.
Service ceiling: 10.5kg.
Absolute ceiling: 13kin.

PROPULSION SYSTEM

The main power unit is a liquid rocket with a pressurized fuel feed and variable automatic thrust.

The following are weights, performance and dimensions of the main unit:

WEIGHTS

Main power fuel (Tonka):12.7 kg.
Main power oxidizer (Salbei): 59.2kg.
Compressed air. 3.0kg.
Charged weight: 159.0kg.
Weight empty: 80.0kg.

PERFORMANCE:

Total launching impulse: 14,000 kg. /sec.
Main thrust unit impulse: 12,500 kg. /sec.
Total impulse: 26,500 kg. /sec.
Launching thrust (see Operating Technique) 3,500 kg, /sec.
Maximum thrust of main unit: 380kg.
Minimum thrust of main unit: 60kg.
Burning time of main unit: 40-90 sec.
Maximum combustion chamber pressure: 40atm.
Average thrust: 220kg.
Average time of burning: 57 sec.

DIMENSIONS (COMBUSTION CHAMBER)

Overall length of main thrust unit: 17in.
Overall diameter: 4.5in,
Throat of nozzle diameter: 1.6in,
Exit of nozzle diameter: 2.88in.

OPERATING AND OPERATIONAL TECHNIQUE OF THE Hs117 PROPULSION SYSTEM.

Because aerodynamic characteristics at high speed change rapidly with small changes in speed, to make the control problems as simple as possible, it was decided that the speed of the missile should be held as nearly constant throughout the flight, as was practicable. This was accomplished by automatically regulating the thrust output of the main jet, in relation to the velocity of the missile, 240m/sec. being the arbitrary, average velocity. This regulation was accomplished by balancing the two pressures taken from a pitot static tube across two opposed aneroid barometric elements which, in turn, by means of electrical contacts, actuate an electric motor which operates a fuel control valve, limiting the flow of fuel to the combustion chamber. A constant proportion of the two reactants entering the combustion chamber must be maintained at all times, at a ratio of 2 parts nitric acid to 1 part hydrocarbon. If one or the other of the reactants is allowed to collect in the combustion chamber, an explosion will occur. The nitric acid is also used to cool the nozzle. It flows into the cooling jacket at the after end of the nozzle and then flows forward and enters the combustion chamber where it meets the hydrocarbon. No ignition apparatus is necessary, as these two fuels are self-igniting. Professor Wagner was not satisfied with the motors, which were developed by Dr. Sbyrowsky of BMW, feeling that they were too heavy. Dr. Conrad, of the Berlin Technical High School, was employed by BMW to improve the motor design.

Dr. Conrad was experimenting with uncooled liquid fuel motors for this project and at least two forms of combustion chamber material had been tried; one a form of graphite and the other a material built up of many layers of a very pure ceramic material, such as silica or alumina. These showed considerable promise and might have been incorporated in later designs. Other liquid fuels were also being considered. By means of various refinements, it was hoped that the missile speed could be raised from Mach 0.75 to 0.8.

Both reactant tanks were built of aluminium and were carefully machined. The outside casting was bored so that a closely fitting piston (without rings) would slide in it. In operation, the liquid side of the tank was initially full, forcing the piston against the head. As air enters the head, the piston travels to the right, forcing liquid out of the tank. The object of this design was to ensure that, when the tanks were less than half full, no slugs of compressed air were fed down the reactant pipes as the aircraft performs tight manoeuvers. Although the motor would re-ignite after stopping, a collection of one of the two reactants would cause an explosion. On the forward side of the air bottle was a connection, to which was tied a filling plug and pressure gauge which read up to 250 kg/sq. cm. The bottle was charged with air to 220 atms. On the aft connection to the bottle was a diaphragm, which was punctured by an electrically fired squib. The outlet from this connection leads to a regulator, which delivers air to the two reactant tanks at 40 atms. (590lbs./sq.in.) On each side of each reactant tank there was a diaphragm valve, which was blown when the 40 atms. pressure appeared at that point. This was done to prevent any possible contact of the reactants during storage or handling and also to ensure that both fuels entered the combustion chamber at the same time, in order to prevent an explosion. At full thrust, nitric acid entered the combustion chamber through 16 holes and the hydrocarbon through 8 holes of equal size. The thrust regulation was obtained by the aforementioned regulator motor, operating (through a gear train) a rotary valve plate which blocks off the holes, limiting the amount of fuel which can enter the combustion chamber (fuel pressure being constant) and also maintaining the fuel ratio of 2 to 1.

INTELLIGENCE AND CONTROL SYSTEM (ELECTRICAL); TYPE AND DESCRIPTION

This missile at first mounted a Friesicke & Hoptner receiver, which operated at about 6m. The equipment was considered as too complicated and heavy for the missile and consequently was superseded by a further development of the “Stare” radio receiver for the Hs293. This new receiver was of the super-regenerative type, having a much smaller form factor than the previous Hs293 receiver and was designated the E230-3. For controlling the missile, the controlling ground station sends out a high-frequency signal which, by modulation with a lower frequency and appropriate keys, conveyed to the missile directions for altitude, or elevation and azimuth. By using its gyro, the missile is able to interpret and follow these signals. On the ground, the signals are manually initiated by means of a "joystick" control, which sets the pitch and yaw directions for the missile to follow and which the missile will follow, until the position of the stick was changed. On the ground, the courses of the target and the missile are followed by means of an optical sighting device. From observations with this device, missile course corrections are set which brings it to the target. No homing devices had been applied to this missile, although they had been discussed and were under development in several firms. Professor Peterson of AEG had been working for some time on a universal radar ground computer for guiding flak missiles to their target. RIM wanted Wagner to incorporate this in the Hs117 control, but he wished to keep it in its original, simple state. In the future, he intended to develop homing devices, to supplement his visual control, for use in adverse weather conditions. It was reported that Wagner would have liked to have this missile beam guided to a radar following target, but he felt that German radar was too inaccurate for the job. Various developments for the radio control of this missile were being carried out by several firms, some work being done in the range from 20 to 40cm. These frequencies were desirable, because they could be beamed and were less interfered with than the longer wavelengths. Shorter wavelengths were not considered, because suitable tubes had not been developed. In some cases, jet interference could be reduced by changing re-actants. In all cases, solid powder gave the most trouble.

It was considered that Telefunken was doing the best work in radio control; they were concentrating on 40cm. The electrical power for this missile was delivered by a propeller-driven generator, located in one of the two noses of the missile. On the ground, before launching, this same generator was driven by a motor in an outside power source. During this period, the propeller did not turn, as it was provided with a three ball bearing free-wheeling device. The missile was stabilized about its longitudinal axis, by only one gyro.

LIMITATIONS OF THE CONTROL SYSTEM AND MISSILE

The only apparent limitation of this missile lies in the fact that it cannot be seen and consequently, followed in overcast weather. If homing devices, other than optical, were incorporated, this limitation would no longer have existed.

WARHEAD AND FUSE

WARHEAD. Considerable divergence of opinion existed in the RIM on the effectiveness of warheads with blast effect only, as against fragmentation, or incendiary pellet filling, but when the tests of the Hs 117 had been completed in the summer of 1944, the first series was ordered in August of that year, with a blast effect warhead weighing 25kg, filled with "Trialen", which was manufactured by Westfälisch-Anhaltische Sprengstoff-Actien-Gesellschaft (WASAG) at Reinsdorf near Wittenberg.

FUSE. It was intended to use a proximity fuse, whenever developed and available. The performance specifications for the fuse required operation between 6 to 10 metres. It was intended that a small clockwork arming device would arm the missile about 10 seconds after take-off. Another device was incorporated, probably working off the control gyro, which exploded the main charge if the missile rolled over on its back in flight, in which case all controls would be reversed, making the missile uncontrollable from the ground by an operator, who would not be aware of this condition. Another timing device was incorporated, which operated 120 seconds after launching, to destroy the missile.

AUXILIARY EQUIPMENT FOR THE MISSILE.

This missile was equipped with two assisted take off units, one above and one below the fuselage, each provided with nozzles offset at an angle, such that the lines of thrust intersected at about the C. G. of the aircraft. In launching, the lower booster was fired first, thus forcing the missile upward and forward off the launcher, which was a simple, two-armed cradle supporting the missile at the wing roots (zero length rails). There was a 2.5 metre firing lanyard, which fired the top unit automatically. Both units then burned until their powder was used up, by which time the main jet had been ignited and took over. Each assisted take-off unit had a total weight of 90kg and contained 40kg of powder charge. Burning took place from the inside out only, since the outside was treated with "Polygon", a plastic preparation, which prevented burning on the surfaces to which it was applied. The booster thrust totalled 3500lbs, lasting for about 4 seconds. It burned at a rate of about 5.8 grams per sec. This thrust brought the missile up to a speed of about 240m/sec. These booster units were known as SG

(Schmidding Geraet) 33. They were developed by Schmidding in Bodenbach and used powder made by Wasag, located near Wittenberg. At the end of the booster burning time, the boosters were jettisoned by means of a power charge and piston device. Also under discussion was a method of dropping the boosters with a device which depended upon the reduction of the pressure within the booster unit itself.

LAUNCHING DEVICE. This missile was launched from a simple, two-armed cradle, which supported each wing at its root, in such a way that an upward and forward motion of the projectile would carry it free from the launcher. There was no moveable dolly on this launcher. The launcher was manually aimed in elevation and azimuth, in response to signals received from a fire-control point. Sighting devices for the launcher were contemplated, but were never incorporated.

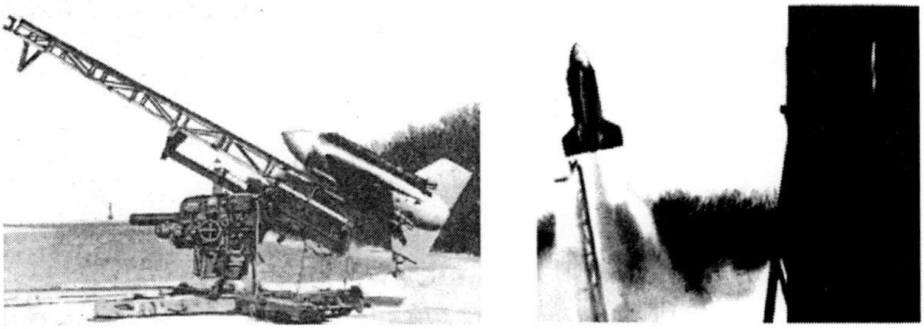

Enzian

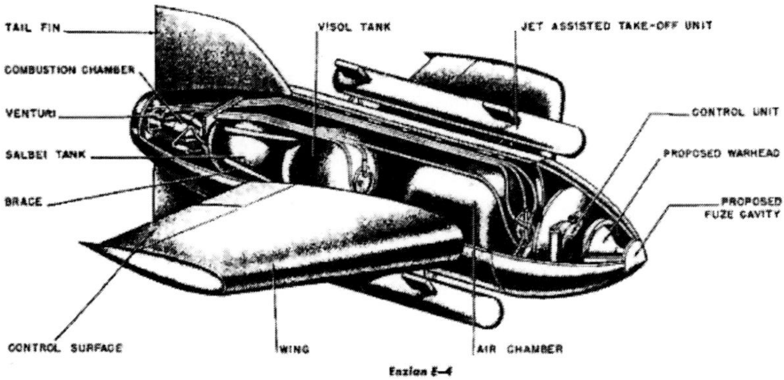

Allied intelligence drawing of Enzian

The Enzian*,* named after a pretty blue flower, was a short, fat rocket, fired from an altered 88mm Flak-type carriage, while the *Hs 117* was a thinner, small rocket, similarly launched. Enzian was developed by the Oberbayerische Forschungsanstalt Oberammergau by Dr Conrad in the workshops of the firm Holzbau GmbH in Sonthofen. Its shape was derived from the Me163 and it was principally made out of wood. It was built as a flying-wing missile, with a forward rise of 30 degrees, one pair of rudders and a wing span of ten metres. The side fins were rigid. Take-off weight was 1965 kilogrammes. Enzian was fired from a sloping platform by four starting rockets of 7000 kilogrammes thrust, which burned for four seconds, before being dropped. This gave Enzian a speed of roughly 540mph. The power unit was the Walter unit which had been used previously. Dr Konrad developed a more efficient unit, which used vinyl-nitric acid as a fuel. After the starting rockets dropped away, the internal motor fired, giving Enzian a thrust of two tons which burned for 70 seconds. The peak altitude was 44500 feet and it had a radius of action of 44000 yards. 38 test flights were made before the wars end. Progress of this missile was hampered when its development was placed in the hands of the SS in November 1944. All work on Enzian ceased, early in 1945.

INTELLIGENCE REPORT

DESCRIPTION. The Enzian was conceived as a ground to air flak weapon. Its secondary purpose was that of an air-to-air weapon. Models E-1, E-2and E-3 were the test and experimental articles. All flight tests were carried out with the E-1. The E-4 was the production design, using an improved rocket motor, designed by Dr. Conrad, instead of the Walter bi-liquid motor used in the earlier designs. The E-4 was a flying-wing design, strikingly similar to the Me163. Its total weight was 1800kg, which included 320kg of the four assisted take-off units. The warhead weight was 500kg. The aircraft was constructed of wood, having an overall length and span of four metres. It attained its velocity of 300 m/sec, with a main thrust unit delivering 2000 kilograms initially, decreasing to 1000kg during the flight. Duration of power was 72 seconds, resulting in a vertical range of 16000 metres and a horizontal range of 25000 metres. The four assisted take-off units delivered a combined thrust of 6000 kilograms for 4 seconds, giving the missile an end speed of 24 m/sec and an acceleration of 3.6g from a launching ramp 6.8 metres in length. The assisted take-off units were jettisoned after 5 seconds. Although it was anticipated that F-4 would be used as an air-to-air weapon with slight modification, mainly by reducing the fuel load, all experimental flight testing had been done from ground to air. A standard 88mm gun carriage was adapted for use as a launching platform, by the simple addition of two iron rails 6.8 metres long. A traverse of 360° and a vertical firing arc from 0° to 85° was obtained. Air launching of the device was routine; i.e., dropping free from underneath the parent aircraft, flying in the direction of the target. The speed on leaving the launching rails was 24m/sec. To avoid the possibility of stalling, no control was applied until the flying speed had reached approximately 55 m/sec. For practical purposes, an elapsed time of 5 seconds was allowed between the triggering of the launching mechanism and the first control signal. The Enzian was directed to the target by radio control, as were practically all German guided missiles. When the target approach was within the range of the homing device, the latter took charge of the missile's final run-in. Coincidence, or line of sight navigation, was used under favourable conditions; however, several methods were accepted for night or reduced visibility use.

AIRFRAME: The Enzian E-4 airframe was a flying wing type, having no horizontal stabilizer and a fixed vertical fin. Control was effected through trailing edge, flaps which acted together as elevators and, differentially, as ailerons. The basic dimensions were as follows:
Length: 4 metres.
Span: 4 metres.
Maximum diameter, fuselage (Circular cross section): 0.88metres.
Root thickness: 20 percent root chord.
Tip thickness: 10 percent root chord.
Wing area: 5square metres.
Aerofoil: NACA symmetrical; no twist.
Dihedral: Zero.
Chord root: 1.25metres.
Chord tip: 0.98 meter.
Sweepback: 30°.
Weight E-4 complete: 1800kg.
Empty (including Warhead): 833kg.
Warhead: 500kg.
Motor: 97kg.
Fuel: 550kg.
Assisted take-off units: 320kg.
Airframe, Including Control Gear: 333kg.
For the purposes of an air-to-air missile, the fuel weight was reduced to 150kg and the assisted take-off units discarded. The airframe was designed to be built of wood, because of metal shortages, but provisions were made for conversion to metal stampings. The production process was to use hot plate gluing methods for fabricating a pressed or plywood material.

AERODYNAMIC PECULIARITIES AND CHARACTERISTICS

Aerodynamically, the E-4 appears conventional. Its stability in flight tests was accepted as good. The E-4s design performance follows:
Maximum velocity (design): 300m/sec,
(Measured Walter motor): 240m/sec.
End speed launching: 24m/sec.
Minimum speed for safe control: 55m/sec.
Vertical range: 16000metres.
(Measured Walter motor): 7000metres.

Horizontal range: 25000metres.
Turning radius: 500metres.
PROPULSION UNIT. Although the Walter power plant was originally intended for the Enzian and was used in the test flights, it was entirely unsatisfactory and was replaced by the Conrad motor. Combustion chamber: 24 kg. Air bottle: 19 kg. Spherical tank: 30 kg

ROCKETS

The bi-fuel liquid rocket motor uses Salbei (92% HNO, +8% H2SO.) and Visol, the ratio of weights being 1.4 to 1. The total quantity of fuel, 550kg, was exhausted in 72 seconds, during which time the thrust was reduced from its initial 2000 to 1000 kg at end of burning. As pressure reduction between the air bottle and liquid tanks was through a simple orifice plate, the progressive reduction in the combustion chamber operating pressure was the direct result of the air bottle's gradual exhaustion. Equal pressure was applied to both liquids and metering was effected by the resistance of the connecting pipes and not that of the nozzles. The total impulse (108000-110000 kg/sec) corresponds to a mean S.I. of 199; however, Wurster stated that the mean propellant consumption of 5.5gm/kg sec rose to 5.6 at start and end of the burning operation and that the S.I. is, of consequence, approximately 182. Although the mixture, Salbei and Visol, was spontaneously inflammable, the Enzian motor used an electrically ignited powder starter in the combustion chamber to effect ignition. This system had the advantage of smoother ignition and less risk of explosion than spontaneous combustion. A further precaution against explosion was taken, by starting the Salbei feed first, by shortening its supply pipes and setting its bursting disks at slightly lower pressure than those of the Visol system. The propulsion unit's arrangement, was dictated by C. G. considerations, as follows: - (1) Air bottle; (2) Visol tank; (3) Salbei tank; (4) combustion chamber. The air flask was originally inflated to a pressure of 200 atm. The liquids were retained in their tanks by means of bursting disks, selected to rupture at 15 atmospheres at entry and 36 atmospheres at exit. All tanks were made of mild steel, 2 mm thick and no corrosion treatment, enamel, or protective coating was employed, as the only General Staff requirement was that the containers should withstand 6 months storage, after being filled with

Salbei and fuel. The weights of component parts of the motor were as follows:-

Combustion chamber: 24 kg. Air bottle: 19 kg. Spherical tank: 30 kg Spherical tank: 24 kg; 97 kg. Fuel weight: 550 kg. Effective S. I. Fuel and Motor= 199x654570 =170, relative to use of an air pressure fuel feed system versus a turbine-pump system. Wursler stated that, according to German figures, the former was lighter up to impulses of 200000 kg/secs and had the additional important advantage of requiring no time for running up to speed. He cited the Me163, which requires 4-5 seconds to run the turbine up to its operational speed of 30000 rpm, pointing out that such delay is prohibitive for a flak rocket.

INTELLIGENCE AND CONTROL SYSTEMS

Operationally, it was expected to use the Enzian in the following manner: - Launch it towards and direct it to the target vicinity, under radio control, using the new German equipment "Kogge" and either line of sight or radar navigation. When the missile's approach to the target came within the operating range of the particular self-seeking head employed, the latter would assume control and direct the Enzian to the target's proximity, on a modified homing course. The proximity fuse, at a pre-determined distance, activated the warhead, which was designed to ensure maximum coverage and effective damage to the target from 45 metres. It was considered pertinent to note here that the Germans were doing extensive research work on the theory of homing courses. Their principal investigations appeared to be based on compromises, lying between a pure chaser or homing course and a straight interception route, procured by interjecting self-navigation into the intelligence system. Initial planning provided for the Enzian's use of one of several types of homing device and proximity fuses currently being developed, or combinations of the above. Tests had not progressed beyond operation with the standard German radio control, the 6 metre "Strassfurg-Kehl," developed by Telefunken and Strassfurt Rundfunk. The "Kogge", designed by Telefunken to operate on a 24 cm wavelength was destined for use in the production Enzians. The I.R. device, "Madrid," developed by Kepka of Vienna, an acoustic device developed by Telefunken and Messerschmitt, or an electronic device was projected for use as homing heads. These articles had been laboratory tested by their manufacturers, only as separate entities.

Spherical tank: 24 kg; 97 kg. Fuel weight: 550 kg.

Metamorphosis of the internal control system, from two axis stabilization, involving the use of four gyros, to acceptance of one axis stabilization, using a Horn gyro having two gimbal rings, is outlined above under experimental testing. Standard Siemens electric servos were used to actuate the control surfaces.

WARHEAD AND FUSING. Three types of warhead of equal weight, 500 kilograms, were projected for E-4. The type which seemed to have accrued the most favour among the Messerschmitt engineers and the local flak officers was built up of a metal shell. The shell was lined with cylindrical pellets cast of mild steel, 20 by 30 mm containing, an incendiary core. The explosive cast into the resulting cavity contained a booster charge and fuse in its forward end on the longitudinal axis. Tests of the above type warhead showed that it could be expected to put 1.5 pellets in an area of 1 square metre at a range of 65 metres. The second type of warhead incorporated 550 small rockets driven by gunpowder, which had been developed by one of the SS laboratories and were to be used as part of the armament of the Me262. The rockets were mounted in the warhead to fire forward in a 30° cone, from a maximum range of 300 metres. Their effective range, however, was 550 metres and at that range each rocket was considered capable of destroying a bomber.

The third type of warhead was straight explosive, dependent only on concussion to destroy the target. Both proximity and self-destruction fuses were provided. The proximity fuses were projected on the I. R., Electronic and Acoustic principles; however, the latter had essentially been dropped by the designers, as the maximum range at which the actuating impulse was of sufficient magnitude was too small to derive most effective results from the warhead.

AUXILIARY EQUIPMENT. Four powder jet assisted take-off units delivering a total of 6000 kilograms thrust for 4 seconds, were used to launch the Enzian. The JATOs produced by Rheinmetall-Borsig weighed 80 pounds each. They were attached by explosive bolts which released the cases, by firing at the end of burning. Small wings fitted to the JATOs assisted in their jettisoning.

The electronic guidance for the whole rocket programme was headed by the firm of Telefunken. The specification for the electronic systems was set out as follows: - target locator, steering control of the missiles, AA missile tracking and the possibility of detonating the warhead. Telefunken investigated the possibility of using beams and of beam guidance of a number of rockets at the same time. It was a problem that was impossible to solve and it was decided to provide for separate target locating and AA missile tracking by means of the coinciding method, with a separate remote control system.

A USAAF B-17Flying Fortress being attacked by a ground to air rocket

Early British Research

In the United Kingdom the investigation of high speed aerodynamics and aircraft structures had been left to scientists, at such places as the Royal Aircraft Establishment, Farnborough. The possibility of achieving supersonic flight had introduced a number of new problems, not the least of which had been that of obtaining aerodynamic information throughout the transonic range of speeds. At this stage, new methods of propulsion, in the form of rockets, ramjets and turbo-jets, gave promise of solving the thrust problem and aroused intense interest in compressible aerodynamics.

Experimental work had shown, quite clearly, that existing wind tunnels could not be made to yield useful data at Mach numbers between about 0.9 and 1.2. Supersonic aerodynamic theory was in its infancy and theory for sonic speeds being virtually non-existent, there was thus the need to develop new methods of research for the transonic region. It was apparent, also, that the most immediate need was for information on the behaviour of the drag of wings and bodies. Projectiles such as bullets, shells, rockets and bombs frequently travelled at supersonic speeds and these came under review.

In October 1943, McKinnon-Wood proposed that use be made of the freely-falling model technique, to investigate sonic and transonic speeds. A basic body, some 13½-ft long and 8-in diameter, was used. It was fitted with stabilizing fins and weighed about 1500lb. To this body were attached the test wings and within the body were fitted the instruments to telemeter to a ground station those quantities which would allow the drag of the model to be determined. A problem with this work was that of aiming the model from an altitude of 35000ft, so that it landed at a safe distance from the ground receiving and control station, but at the same time was not so far away, at any moment during the descent, that the telemetering receivers were unable to obtain a satisfactory signal. It was also necessary to determine the position of the model throughout its descent, in order to establish the appropriate atmospheric conditions during the test and to establish the form of the trajectory, for subsequent analysis of the results. Both these problems were overcome by installing at the ground site

SCR.584 radar tracking equipment, together with a specially designed plotting table.

Flight work was begun in December 1944, using a Mosquito Mk. XVI as parent aircraft. Powered by twin Merlin engines, the Mosquito XVIB had the capability of carrying a 4000lb bomb load. As such, it was the ideal choice for the trial, but it had to have its original bomb doors removed, a special cradle installed and new bomb bay doors fitted. For the early tests at Pawlett and Odstone, Mosquito PR Mk. IX, LR479, was used. Since a pressurised cabin was desirable, the equipment was later transferred to Mosquito BXVI, PF543, which was used thereafter throughout the tests at Orfordness and the Scilly Isles. Later still, a second Mosquito BXVI, PF604, which was primarily employed on a somewhat similar type of experiment, was modified to carry models and so formed a reserve for the first aircraft. Unfortunately, Mosquito PR Mk IX, LR479, crashed with the loss of both the aircrew. A replacement was not immediately available and another Mosquito PR Mk. IX was used. Unlike the Mk. XVI, this aircraft had no pressurised cabin and in consequence, long flights at high altitudes were very arduous for the aircrew. Nevertheless, the special bomb crutches and the experimental equipment were installed and three dummy models, i.e., ones without wings and telemetering equipment, were released from this particular aircraft, to develop the technique. Difficulties experienced in the radar tracking of the mainly wooden aircraft were overcome by applying an aluminium spray finish, which provided a metallic reflecting surface for radar tracking. A tubular framework, attached to the aircraft centre-section, inside the bomb-bay, supported the model on a bomb slip, the jaws of which protruded below the closed bomb doors. The model was thus slung external to the aircraft, being steadied by fore-and-aft crutch pads in the normal manner. An automatic observer was fitted in the aircraft, to record the air speed, altitude and air temperature when the model was released. A separate electrical supply was carried in the aircraft, so that telemetering transmissions could be made from the model from a source of known constant voltage prior to release, without causing any drain on the batteries carried within the model.

The de Havilland Mosquito

Mosquito with a free fall model mounted externally

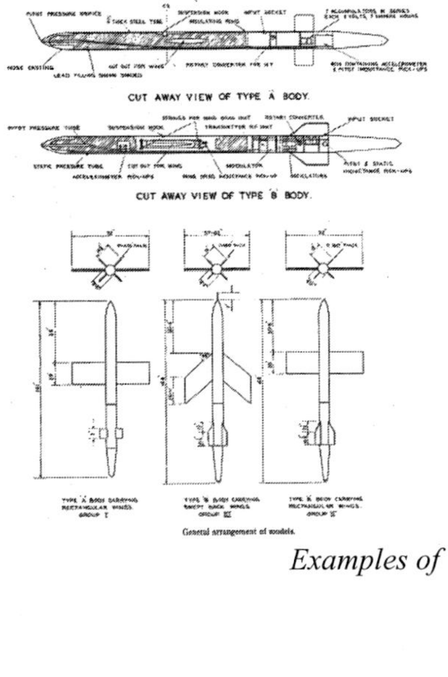

General arrangement of models.

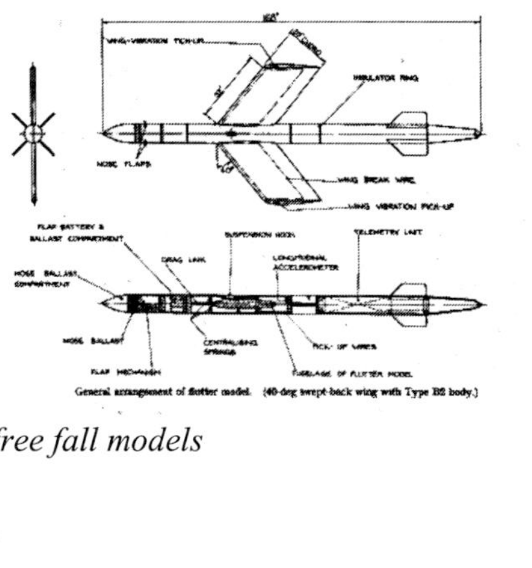

General arrangement of flutter model. (40-deg swept-back wing with Type B2 body.)

Examples of the free fall models

A series of flights was made by PF543 and PF604, to determine the errors in their altimeters and air speed indicators, due to the position of the static vent. The aircraft thermometers were also calibrated to determine the error due to compressibility. The first two dummy models were released at Pawlett range in Somerset in July/August 1945. Pawlett range was closed down shortly afterwards and the work transferred to Odstone range in Berkshire, where the third dummy model was released in September of the same year. On this occasion icing-up of the bomb-slip caused a temporary "hang-up" and the model fell away some seconds late; it landed outside the range and caused some minor damage to private property. Following this incident, it was decided to transfer the work to Orfordness range in Suffolk, where the models could be dropped into the sea.

By August 1946, three dummy models had been released at Orfordness for training purposes and to prove the ground equipment. During the following two months, four further models were released. Of the latter, which carried two-channel telemetering equipment, one model was a basic body without wings and the other three had rectangular wings of biconvex section and thickness/chord ratios of 12 per cent, 8 per cent and 5 per cent respectively.

In 1946, the group which had been engaged on this freely falling model work, was called upon to extend its activities to cover work on rocket test vehicles, air-launched from a parent aircraft. Orfordness was unsuitable for this new work, because of shipping traffic in adjoining waters and its proximity to populated areas. A search was made for a site which would fulfil the requirements of both experiments and one was eventually found at the Scilly Isles. This group of islands was located in the Atlantic, some 28 miles W.S.W. of Lands End. The largest of the group, St. Mary's Island, was chosen as a site for the ground equipment. By mid-1947, the installation work was complete and improvements, based on the lessons learned at the previous ranges, were incorporated. G.C.I. (ground-controlled interception) radar equipment existing at this site was of great value in assisting the SCR.584 operator to locate and hold his target (the parent aircraft). The method of tying together the time of operation of the various cameras and recording apparatus was greatly improved. Thereafter, six-channel telemetering equipment was employed.

The first model was released at the Scilly Isles range in August 1947 and was followed by two more before the end of the year. Of these, the first two were dummies, to check the new ground station set-up and to train new members of the ground crew, while the third was a test model fitted with rectangular wings of biconvex section and six-channel telemetering equipment. On a number of occasions, wooden dummy models without wings were released, mainly to check radar functioning and to further develop the operational technique. They were much lighter than the telemetering models and consequently did not reach the same speed.

At Farnborough, was an example of the captured German ground to air missile, Schmetterling. With the cancellation of the Miles supersonic project, it was felt by the Air Ministry that it would be a waste to lose all the supersonic test data and it was therefore decided to take a further step towards supersonic speed. A contract was placed with Vickers-Armstrongs Ltd for a small, supersonic missile, which was to be a scale model of the M.52 and be powered by a rocket motor. Initially, Vickers had intended using a solid fuel rocket motor, which built up its thrust through a system of pipes, leading to a single venturi in the tail. But with the availability of all the German rocket details from the Me163 and missiles, such as Schmetterling, it was felt prudent to merge all the technology and drop the solid fuel rocket completely. The scientists at Vickers, under the leadership of Barnes Wallis and those of the Air Ministry, believed that they could resurrect the Miles project of 1943 and go much further. As an insurance against the failure of the Miles M.52 with the W.2/700, Miles had already projected a version with a Walter rocket motor. Carried in the belly of a Lancaster, the rocket M.52 would have been taken to 31000ft and then released. After its test flight, the M.52 would have glided onto the sea and been recovered by a ship, equipped with a special crane. Possibly some of the Miles data was incorporated into the Vickers-Supermarine Attacker, because there was some similarity between the Attacker and the M.52 in the shape of the fuselage.

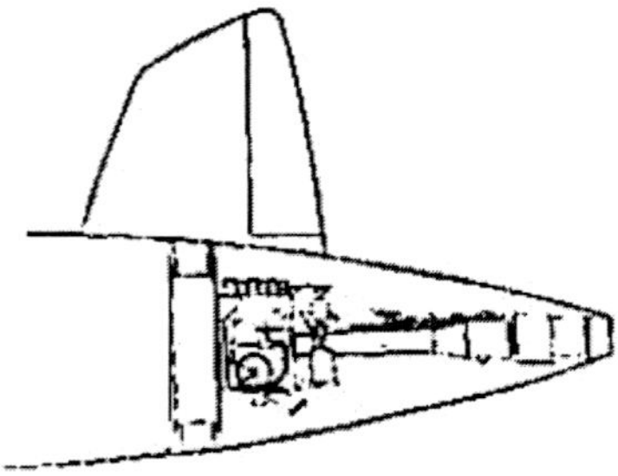

Miles M.52 fitted with a Walter rocket motor

A post – war display of the M.52 air-dropped model.

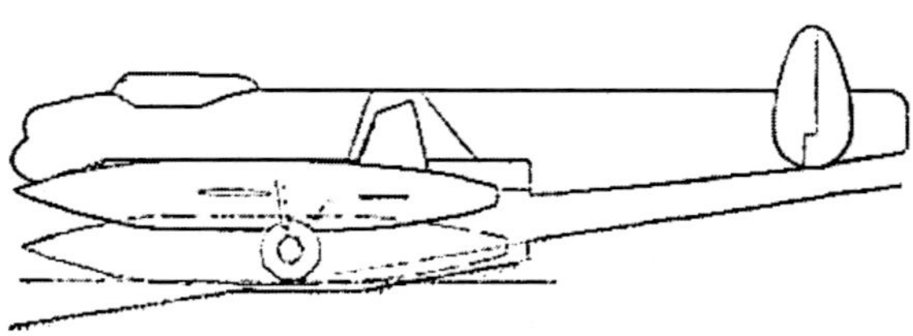

The M.52 and proposed Lancaster mother plane

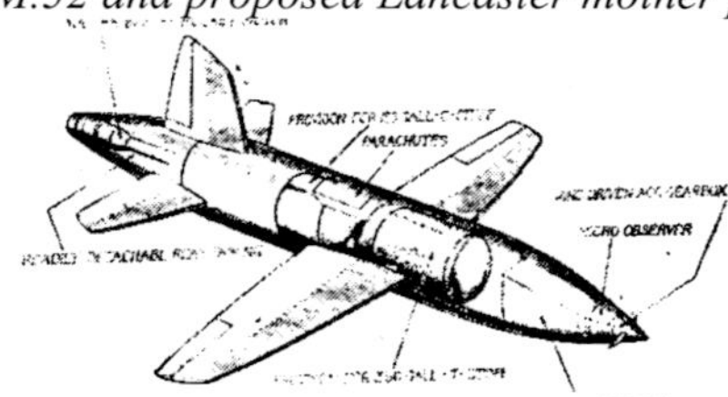

One of the M.52 models with a Walter rocket motor

The Vickers model was a 3/10 scale model of the M.52, but without the air intake behind the cockpit. It was to be built around a rocket motor, with the wing being one-piece mahogany. Inside the fuselage were a two-axis automatic control unit and a radio telemetering installation. The all-moving tailplane was once again made of mahogany and carried a two-bearing shaft, bolted onto the model's structure. In the nose was a large balance weight and a fuel tank, while in the tail another fuel tank was installed, with the rocket motor at the rear. Underneath the wing, in a fuselage compartment, was the electronics suite, including an automatic pilot.

Design of the model commenced in 1945 and by September 1946, was being exhibited at many aviation venues, such as the first post - war display at Farnborough, but by 1948 it was much more than a mere curio; it had become a complex test vehicle, which could be air launched from an aeroplane at 36000ft and operate under its own guidance system. The progress with the design was all the more successful and remarkable, due to the combination of the British airframe with German rocket technology.

The Air Ministry had ordered twelve Vickers models and each one was prefixed by the letter "A". Because of the pioneering nature of the tests models, A8 and A9 were used for early flight trials with the new Walter rocket motor, as copied from the Germans. At the end of February 1948, a Mosquito dropped A9 from an altitude of 35000ft on the first rocket motor starting test. After it was dropped, the rocket motor ignited for about ten seconds and the model fell into the sea. The second trial with A8 took place on 5th March 1948 and once again took place at the same altitude, but the motor failed to ignite. Another three models, A10, A11 and A12, were now allocated to the motor trials. A12 and A10 were released successfully from an altitude of 25000ft, while A11 exploded just after release. These tests revealed a weakness in the Walter rocket motor, which was traced to the fuel pipes failing at low temperatures. The pipework had to be replaced by aluminium and stainless steel. Another weakness was traced to the rocket motor, when it was found that ignition was very difficult to obtain at altitude and the RAE had to embark on a sub-sidiary test programme to resolve this.

Another delay was encountered, when it was found that many of the British personnel had little experience in working with liquid-fuelled rockets and German scientists had to be brought in to help. All these faults had come to light when model A2 was on test at Saint Eval, Cornwall. A Mosquito was loaded up with A2 and fuelled the night before the test flight was due to take place. In the morning, when the model was checked, it was found that the rocket motor chamber had been contaminated with fuel, due to leaking seals. After a few hours, the fault was rectified and the Mosquito readied for flight. When A2 was released from the Mosquito, there was a small explosion inside the model's fuselage; A2 rolled onto its back, then blew up. New tests were made on the rocket motor at Farnborough and it was discovered that there was a fault in the low pressure side of the motor with the fuels failing to ignite spontaneously. The motor problem was finally overcome by fitting an ignitor inside the combustion chamber, which burned with a continuous flame. The ignitor now ensured that the fuels burned with the same chemical combination, inside the combustion chamber.

Vickers now gave the model a speed of about Mach 1.3 at altitude and planned that it should be launched at a true airspeed of 400 mph. at 36000ft. With these requirements in mind, the choice of a suitable aeroplane to carry the model was finally narrowed down to the Mosquito XVIB, which had already been used for supersonic model work. The bomb doors were cut away, so that they could open and close with the model in position. The model was installed just inside the bomb bay and slightly proud of the fuselage. Recording the results was an Air Ministry priority and the Mosquito was fitted with a whole suite of cameras. Inside the rear fuselage camera bay, an automatic observer was fitted, together with an F24 camera. In the port engine nacelle a 35mm Vinten camera was installed, giving a three quarter view of the model as it was released. Inside the Mosquito's nose, two further Vinten cameras were installed, which were mounted at 45¼ degree angle and could record the final stages of the model's flight. In addition to the three Vinten cameras and the F24 camera, the Crown Film Unit had installed its own Vinten camera inside the rear camera bay of the Mosquito.

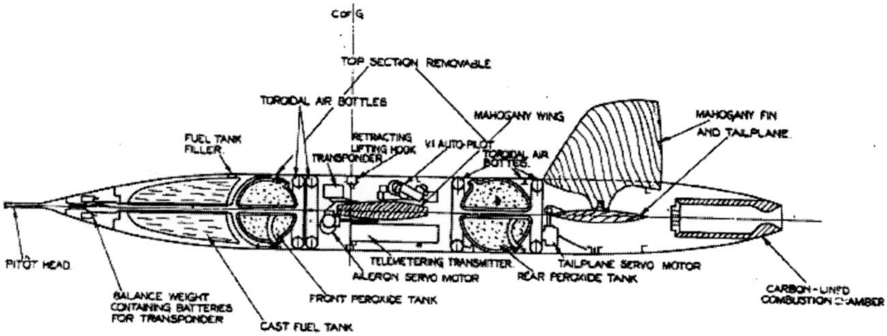

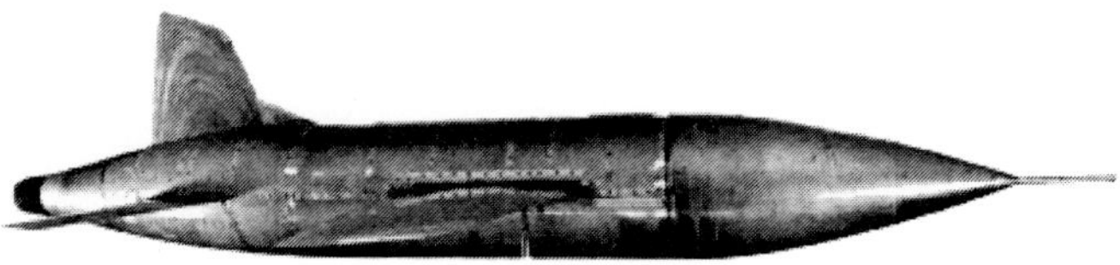

Vickers Trans-Sonic Missile rocket model

Upper and lower centre section

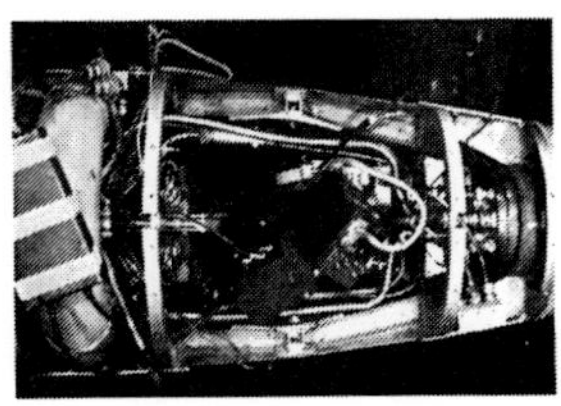

Upper and lower tail

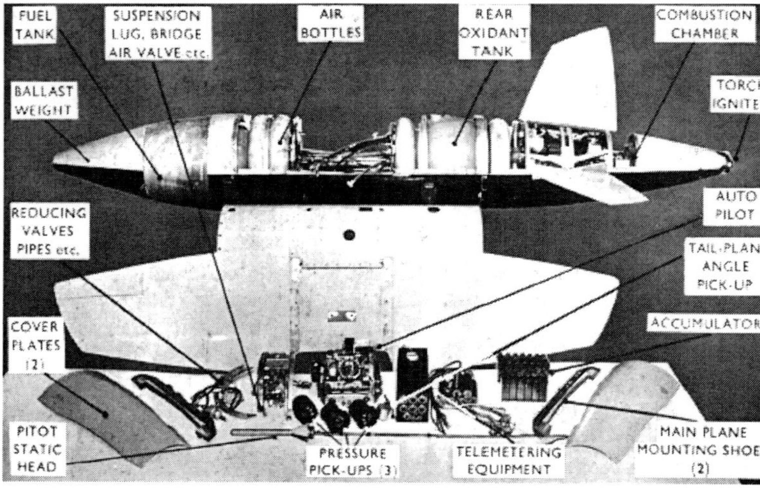

Trans-Sonic Missile breakdown

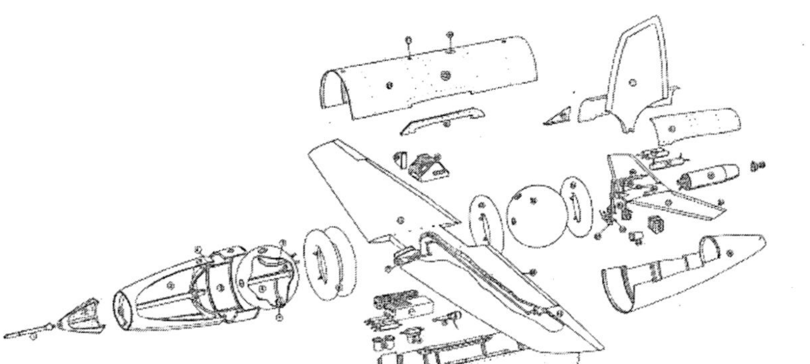

FIG. 23. The R.A.E.-Vickers transonic rocket model.

RAE breakdown of the model

Though the parent aircraft was well equipped with cameras to record the flight of the model, a Gloster Meteor IV was provided as camera chase plane, to cover the release stages of the flight. The Meteor was fitted with five forward facing G.S.A.P. 9mm cameras, housed in the gun positions and all armament was deleted. The trial was to have been controlled using S.C.R., but during early formation flights with the two aircraft, the radar operators tended to lock onto the Meteor and largely ignore the very faint blip of the all-wood Mosquito. Another problem was discovered in trying to formate at such high altitudes; the pilots were expected to find each other by the aircrafts' contrails. As an insurance against formation failure, the Mosquito had four smoke generators fitted to the wing tank mountings. In ground tests one generator produced a considerable amount of smoke, but when used in the rarefied atmosphere at 36000ft, the results from all four smoke generators proved to be very disappointing.

While the missile was being readied for flight at St. Eval, the R.A.E./Vickers team was sent an urgent and priority signal from the Air Ministry; it had been decided that the test flight of A3 was to be the final and only flight of the trans-sonic model. The Air Ministry had decided that, although a vast amount of experience had been gained from the trials of the rocket motors and the guidance systems, the amount of time and financial input for just one flight did not justify any more expenditure and the contract was to be cancelled. On 9th October 1948, the model, painted a high gloss yellow [upper surfaces] and gloss black [lower surfaces], was readied for its flight. A Lancaster from St. Mawgan was detailed to report any shipping movements and warn vessels that a trial was taking place. Flying at around 35000ft and at just less than Mach 0.5, the Mosquito released A3 cleanly. After six seconds the rocket motor ignited and accelerated the model smoothly to a speed of Mach 1.4. After seven minutes flight time, it was estimated that A3 had travelled about sixty miles and then fallen into the sea.

Although this first and only trial of a complete model was a success, radar difficulty concerning the size of the blips and the operator's inability to identify the Mosquito, the model and the Meteor, meant that there was no true plot of the model's course. The tests also revealed that the performance of the jet-propelled Meteor was far superior to that of the piston-engined Mosquito. (The Meteor always took off twenty minutes after the Mosquito.)

Technically, the initial construction of the rocket motor and its ignition system had to rely on German data, but with ingenuity, the British scientists cured the ignition problem and the faults with the Walter rocket motor. There was never really any official enthusiasm for the project from the Air Ministry, which felt that the M.52, Vickers Armstrongs and the German combination were just aeronautical oddities.

Mosquito trials aircraft with the Vickers Trans-Sonic model

Stand Off

The discovery, in early 1939, of neutron-induced fission in uranium, immediately prompted investigation in the United Kingdom, not only of a controlled fission chain reaction, but also of an uncontrolled, explosive chain reaction. Although official British circles viewed, with a high degree of scepticism, the possible significance of uranium fission for military application, some research was initiated at British universities on the theoretical aspects of achieving an explosive reaction. Progress was slow, the initial results were discouraging and following the outbreak of World War II, the effort was reduced and resources were moved to more pressing and more promising defence projects. The turning point came in March 1940, with the inspired memorandum by O. R. Frisch and R. E. Peierls, then both of Birmingham University, in which they predicted that a reasonably small mass of pure uranium 235 would support a fast chain reaction and outlined a method by which uranium 235 might be assembled in a weapon. The importance of the Frisch-Peierls memorandum was recognised with surprising rapidity and a uranium subcommittee of the Committee for the Scientific Survey of Air Warfare was set up. This subcommittee was soon to assume an independent existence as the MAUD Committee

As France fell, two scientists, Hans von Halban and Lew Kowarski, escaped to England. They came from a Paris-based team that had been the first to report, early in 1939, the possibility of achieving a slow chain reaction in ordinary uranium 235. Even though scientists believed, by 1940, that this slow reaction would be useless for a bomb, it held out the hope of nuclear power. The two French physicists carried with them to Britain the total world stock of heavy water, which they had brought from France. Heavy water was the best known and most efficient moderator for slowing down neutrons. The French scientists settled at the Cavendish Laboratory in Cambridge and here two of their colleagues predicted that, in the course of slow chain reactions in ordinary, unseparated uranium, a new element, almost completely unknown in nature, would be formed, which would behave like uranium 235 and would be useable for weapons. This was the element, later called Plutonium.

The Maud Committee, fearful of possible German scientific progress, worked with frantic haste. The committee then produced two reports on its work at the end of July 1941. These reports, "Use of Uranium for a Bomb" and "Use of Uranium as a Source of Power," were formally processed through the Ministry of Aircraft Production, the high-level Scientific Advisory Committee and the Chiefs of Staff and to Churchill, but as a result of a great deal of unofficial lobbying, he made the decision that the bomb project should proceed before the official recommendations reached him. It was recognised that the project had to be set up on a more formal basis and the "Directorate of Tube Alloys," a title chosen as a cover name, was formed within the Department of Scientific and Industrial Research.

Imperial Chemical Industries Limited agreed to release Mr W. A. Akers to take charge of this Directorate. After Sir John Anderson had ceased to be Lord President and became Chancellor of the Exchequer, Churchill asked him to continue to supervise this work, for which he had special qualifications. To advise him, there was set up, under his chairmanship, a Consultative Council, composed of the President of the Royal Society, the Chairman of the Scientific Advisory Committee of the Cabinet, the Secretary of the Department of Scientific and Industrial Research and Lord Cherwell. The Minister of Aircraft Production, at that time Lord Brabazon, also served on this Committee. Under the Chairmanship of Mr. Akers there was also a Technical Committee, on which sat the scientists who were directing the different sections of the work and some others. This Committee was originally composed of Sir James Chadwick, Professor Peierlsand Drs Halban, Simon and Slade. Later, it was joined by Sir Charles Darwin and Professors Cockcroft, Oliphant and Feather. Full use was also made of university and industrial bodies.

The Maud Report clearly showed the possibility of an atomic bomb, certainly with uranium 235 and possibly with plutonium. It also described the processes and plant required for bomb production, even estimating the cost. A copy of the report was taken to the still neutral United States, where groups of scientists were, rather desultorily, studying bomb possibilities. When they read the Maud

Report, they saw very clearly that production of an atomic bomb was, indeed, possible.

After they received the Maud Report, the Americans really took their project seriously and even before Pearl Harbor, launched what was to be the huge Manhattan Project. Britain was aware that Germany was developing nuclear weapons and the development of such a type of British weapon would also increase Britain's prestige in the world.

Clearly an atomic project would mean an enormous industrial effort by Britain. Was it possible to build the plant in beleaguered Britain, which was under enemy air attack and short of manpower and materials? British scientists and politicians decided that the first pilot plants ought to be built in Britain and later, full-scale plants in North America, preferably in Canada, with American help. But the project had such vast implications that there was a fear of transferring all the work from Britain to the United States, which was still neutral and might become isolationist after the war, as it had done after the 1914-18 war. At the end of 1941, the British were ahead. Then, on October 11th 1941, before America entered the war, President Roosevelt sent Churchill a letter suggesting that efforts be jointly co-ordinated, or even merged. Accordingly, the British and American efforts were joined and all British scientists sent to America under the greatest secrecy.

By the summer of 1942 the Americans had forged ahead very quickly. The British, struggling to build a few pilot units for a uranium separation plant, now wished to be partners in the American project, but they were too late and were not wanted. Even the exchange of information ceased and the British were cut off from all knowledge of the American project. The British now had no security clearance, or had it withdrawn, to receive information on the Manhattan Project.

This situation changed when Vannevar Bush, the director of the Office of Scientific Research and Development and U.S. Secretary of War, Henry Stimson, visited London in July 1943. At a meeting with Churchill, a number of misunderstandings on both sides were satisfactorily resolved and it was decided that the British should draft an agreement, defining the terms for future collaboration on the bomb project. The draft agreement included a statement of the necessity for the bomb project to be a completely joint effort, a pledge that neither country would use the bomb against the other, a further pledge that neither country would use the bomb against or disclose it to a third party, without mutual consent and recognition of the United States' right to limit whatever post-war commercial advantages of the project might accrue to Great Britain. A mission to Washington, by Sir John Anderson, reached agreement on provisions for establishment of a General Policy Committee and for renewal of information exchange.

Winston Churchill and President Franklin D. Roosevelt agreed to sign the Quebec Agreement on 19th August 1943. (There they also discussed Poland, Palestine and the Soviet Union) There was no mention of the Manhattan Project in the declaration, only Tube Alloys. The agreement enabled the British to participate in the Manhattan Project and also to set up arrangements for joint exploitation and purchase of uranium supplies. After the Quebec Agreement, nearly all the British scientists working on uranium 235, or on fast neutrons for bombs, joined the US project. Most went to Los Alamos for Project "Y", to the atomic bomb laboratory in New Mexico. The British contribution to the Manhattan Project was of a high standard and of key importance in most of the crucial areas of research, but the contribution was essential; in fact, all of Tube Alloys was absorbed by the Manhattan Project.

President Roosevelt had endorsed the construction of the atomic bomb in June 1942. Both the United States and Britain were now motivated to develop an atomic bomb before the war's end, due to the fear of Nazi Germany acquiring the weapon first and using it against the Allies. Britain now combined efforts with the United States and Canada to develop the first atomic bomb. By 1943, however, Britain was already behind the United States in technical development and was only able to make "minor contributions".

The increase in Anglo-American cordiality was due almost entirely to the personal relationships built up at the working level. Of pre-eminent importance was the rapport established between General Leslie Richard Groves, jnr., director of the Manhattan Project and Professor James Chadwick, senior technical advisor to the British members of the Combined Policy Committee.

With the resumption of cooperation, the first task was an updating one. The British handed over a pile of reports on the progress of their work and General Groves supplied a copy of the progress report he had just submitted to the President. The British were amazed by the progress made in America and staggered by the scale of the American effort. The estimate of the total project cost was already in excess of one thousand million dollars, compared to the British expenditure in 1943 of only about half a million pounds. Chadwick was in no doubt that the first duty of the British was to assist the Americans with their project and abandon all ideas of a wartime project in England. He concluded that this would be best achieved by sending British scientists to work in the United States. Before the end of 1943, Chadwick, Peierls and M. L. E. Oliphant had taken up indefinite residence in America. Chadwick was occupied mostly in Washington with diplomatic and administrative functions, but spent some time in Los Alamos. Peierls worked initially on gaseous diffusion, but later at Los Alamos. Oliphant, with three colleagues, worked at Berkeley, with Lawrence's electromagnetic team. A further two scientists were attached to Los Alamos. The exodus of British scientists to America accelerated in the early months of 1944. However, those who joined the programme did not stay long and all were withdrawn by the autumn of 1944. The British team which joined Lawrence at Berkeley built up rapidly to about 35 and was completely integrated into the American group; most stayed until the end of the war. The British team, assembled at Los Alamos, finally numbered 19 and, as at Berkeley, the scientists were assigned to existing groups in the Laboratory (although it was said not to those groups concerned with the preparation of plutonium and its chemistry and metallurgy).

The first British scientists to go to Los Alamos were mainly nuclear physicists. They included Frisch, who led the Anglo-American group that first demonstrated the critical mass of uranium 235 and E. Bretscher, who found a niche in the group already thinking about fusion weapons. As the team built up, most of the British scientists were allocated to work on implosion weapon problems and to bomb assembly in general. Implosion was considered before the British arrived at Los Alamos, but Dr. J. L. Tuck made a significant contribution with his suggestion of explosive lenses for the achievement of highly symmetrical implosions. During 1944, Dr. W. G. Penney was recruited to assist with the explosive side of the programme, as were Dr. W. G. Marley and two assistants. Eventually, six British scientists, Bretscher, Frisch, P. B. Moon, Peierls, Penney and G. Placzek became the heads of joint groups and a seventh, Marley, became head of a section. Furthermore, two highly distinguished consultants were made available under British auspices, namely Professor Niels Bohr and Sir Geoffrey Taylor. Bohr's visits to Los Alamos were inspirational and Taylor was able to contribute significantly to the work on hydrodynamics.

There is no objective way of measuring the contribution made by the British to the Manhattan Project at Los Alamos and elsewhere. General Groves often acknowledged the importance of the early work in the United Kingdom and the substantial contribution made by her scientists in America. The British presence, though small in relation to scientific numbers, certainly had a beneficial effect on the Project. The British scientists served a function, not otherwise available, in that closed community, as a centre of second opinions by scientists whose reputations were generally acknowledged.

The British Mission personnel started departing from the laboratory shortly after the Trinity test at Alamogordo Air Base on 16th July 1945, leaving only Ernest Titterton as the British representative in the laboratory until the end of 1946. During the spring and summer of 1946, W. G. Penney, J. L. Tuck and E. W. Titterton served with B Division in Operation Crossroads.

After the Trinity test, atomic weapons were used aggressively against Japan, at Hiroshima and Nagasaki, resulting in Japan's unconditional surrender. But because of the Quebec Agreement, Great Britain gave its explicit consent for the bombings earlier on 4th July 1945.There were two British observers at the Nagasaki operation, Wing Commander Leonard Cheshire V.C. and William G. Penney.

During Operation Crossroads, Dr. W. G. Penney and Sir Geoffrey Maylor brought forward specific proposals for placing major combatant ships in a sort of pentagonal arrangement around the point of aim to improve the range distribution under the random bombing dispersion expected. These proposals, which were substantially accepted, conditioned the grouping, especially within about 1,000 yards. Although the Army Air Forces originally had desired an aircraft carrier as a point-of-aim for the bombing plane, they proposed at this time, that the centre ship should be the heaviest and most resistant ship available. The U.S.S. Pennsylvania was chosen for the central position of the test.

Matters of co-operation were to change when the new president, Harry Truman, (F. D. Roosevelt had died in the spring of 1945) said that the Quebec Agreement was news to him. Washington could not find the agreement and had to request a copy of it from London. Precisely the same thing happened in the case of the aide-memoire signed by Churchill and Roosevelt, in September 1944. Truman cancelled the Quebec Agreement and went along with the consensus in Washington that the United States should work alone on nuclear energy. On 1st August 1946, he signed the McMahon Act, which made it illegal for any American to share nuclear/atomic information with any other country, signalling that the United States was now supremely dominant in the nuclear field. Britain was left to its own devices. Even with technical isolation looming, Anglo-American co-operation continued with Operation Front Line/ Project Ruby in May 1946. "Front Line" was the RAF code. This project was concerned with testing the penetrating power of heavy, giant conventional aerial bombs. The American contribution to Project Ruby was the B-29 Superfortress and the B-17 Flying Fortress. The Superfortress dropped the American manufactured Tallboy and Grand Slam on the old U-Boat pens at Farge, Heligoland and obsolete naval vessels. The B-17 dropped the British Disney Bomb, which was a rocket-propelled penetration bomb. The much-reduced Royal Air Force provided Lancasters of 15 Squadron, with code letters "R," "T," "S," "Z" and "V," etc. carrying the Grand Slam bomb. Another co-operative venture took place with Project Harken, in July 1947, which was a similar test. It had two phases; a British phase and an American Phase. All phases were flown by American aircraft (B-29), because the British no longer had an aircraft capable of carrying a heavy store under test. The purpose of the British phase was to determine the altitude at which the British 1650lb model bomb would break up when striking the target.

B-29 with an American made Grand Slam

Avro Lancaster and B-29 Superfortress used for Operation Ruby/Front Line/Harken, joint Anglo-American bomb trials. The B-29s are shown at RAF Marham

Rocket –powered Disney bomb mounted under a B-17 Flying Fortress

The British bomb performed less well than the American Amazon, fabricated, 22000lb SAP T14 and the fabricated, 12000lb SAP T10, bombs. Cast examples (British) were prone to breaking up on impact. The tests were drawn out, due to the slow supply of the American bombs from the manufacturer, A.O. Smith. There were also engine problems with the B-29, which developed severe vibration over 25000 feet, resulting in the bomb sight coming off true. (The British wanted their store to be dropped from 35000 feet.)

Other bombs adopted by the Americans were the giant aerial bombs, designed by Barnes Wallis. They ranged from 12000lbs, 25000lbs to 44000lbs. The latter was first built in model form in Glasgow at the North British Loco Works. They were carried in the Boeing B-29 and the Convair B-36. A radio-controlled version of the Tallboy, used in the Korean War, was the Tarzon, (an acronym of ***TA***llboy, ***R***ange and a***Z***imuth ***ON***ly). Bell, the major contractor, attached a lift ring to the warhead around the bomb's approximate centre of gravity. Tarzon, measuring twenty-one feet in length, four and a half feet in diameter and with a gross weight of 13,000 pounds, could be dropped only by a specially-modified B-29 Superfortress, with cut-outs in the bomb bay doors and was limited to a single bomb per aircraft sortie. During the Korean War, the 19th Bomb Group modified three B-29s to carry, launch and guide the new missiles. The first Tarzon was dropped in Korea on December 14th, 1950. Over the course of the next four months, a total of thirty Tarzon missions was flown, once again with promising results. In addition to destroying numerous bridges, often knocking out two or three spans with its single mammoth explosion, Tarzon had scored a direct hit on a hydro -electric installation, challenging the conventional wisdom that guided weapons were suitable only for long, narrow targets. Such was its initial success, that the USAF negotiated the production of 1000 Tarzons, but the whole project was terminated due to safety issues when the weapon was dropped at low level.

The America McMahon Act of 1946 forbade any co-operation with other nations on armaments, especially nuclear weapons. This meant that Britain was not to be given access to American nuclear technology, although this did not stop the Americans from using Ministry of Supply data, in its atomic tests of 1947 and at Bikini

Radio-controlled VB-13 Tarzon was designed by Bell around a British 12000lb Tallboy bomb with guidance system by the Radio Corporation of America. It was successfully used by the USAF for destroying bridges during the Korean War.

in 1948. The Americans had requested special test paper, designed by William Penney, to be used in these tests. Penney, who had been present at the Nagasaki operation, had been a key figure in Britain's contribution to the Manhattan Project in the United States. He had also calculated the type of atomic air burst that was to be used against the Japanese and the Americans appreciated his knowledge. Penney had become assistant professor of mathematics at Imperial College, London, at the early age of 27 and during the war he worked for the Home Office on the effects of high explosives and for the Admiralty on the effects of waves on the transportable Mulberry harbours used in the Allied invasion of Europe. In 1944 he went to Los Alamos and became a key member of its staff on the Manhattan Project. In 1946 he was invited to take part in the US bomb tests at Bikini Atoll. The Americans made several unsuccessful attempts to persuade him to leave Britain and work in the United States. He got on extremely well with the Americans, who found him entirely honest and unassuming. During the Bikini tests, two British Canberra bombers were used to take air samples. Flown by Royal Air Force crews, the two bombers had all their British markings removed and replaced by U.S. markings.

In November 1944, the British chiefs of Staff had requested that a committee be set up to investigate methods of warfare and future weapons. This committee was headed by Sir Henry Tizard. The committee reported in July 1944 and foresaw the use of jet aircraft and atomic weapons. At the end of the war and in late 1945, Britain started producing nuclear weapons as a matter of policy, under Prime Minister Clement Attlee. It then became apparent that Britain also wanted a weapon of deterrence against nations which had atomic weapons. From those early days it became clear that nuclear weapons offered Britain two avenues, a weapon of defence and a weapon of deterrence - *"The Attlee Doctrine."* One of the recommendations of the Tizard Report was that the only practical weapons system capable of using an atomic weapon was an aircraft. In December 1945, another committee, "The Advisory Committee on Atomic Energy," recommended that Britain should build two atomic piles for the production of plutonium. By July 1946, an Operational Requirement –OR1001 had been issued for a British atomic bomb. The Air Staff then issued an operational requirement for a four jet bomber, to deliver a 10000lb bomb (atomic) to a target 1500 n.m. away, cruising at 50000 feet, at a speed of 500 knots. This was O.R.229.

On the afternoon of 8th January 1947, the Attlee government had started the independent nuclear weapons programme. Initial studies predicted that nuclear bombs would be utilized for attack. The hope was that, by 1947, the possession of nuclear weapons would be a sufficient defence against such an attack - deterrence. Influenced by a small defence sub-committee of the British cabinet, the GEN75 Committee, which had met in 1946-1947 to consider the nuclear agenda, it was decided that Britain should go ahead with its own nuclear programme for three reasons. Firstly, the subcommittee believed that perceptions of global political influence were intimately related to the possession of nuclear weapons. When advising the British government on the possibilities of building a bomb in the early days of World War II, a scientific advisory committee had noted: "Even if the war should end before the bombs are ready, the effort would not be wasted, since no nation would care to risk being caught without a weapon of such decisive possibilities." This observation has become a basic principle of British defence policy and has frequently been echoed in subsequent government statements on the need for a British deterrent. The second reason for Britain's decision to acquire its own nuclear weapons related to Britain's global interests. Britain felt that it needed nuclear weapons to make a Soviet attack on Western Europe less likely, particularly if its conventional forces were deployed around the world to police the Empire. Thirdly, Britain's leaders feared American isolationism and that she might be left to fend for herself in an increasingly hostile and uncertain international environment.

A British nuclear force was seen as "a hedge against political failure [by the United States]. It was that measure of 'self-defence' which would bring 'mutual aid.' - "*Put another way, British acquisition of nuclear weapons would put a British finger on the American nuclear trigger.*"

B-29 s of the type that were sent to England in 1948. Airfields had already been allocated as early as 1945 by joint RAF/USAAF decisions, with funds being allotted for rebuilding certain airfields for the B-29. Some of these airfields are still in use today.

North American B-45 and RB-45(left). "46", above right, was photographed at Prestwick in 1958.This aircraft was stolen and crashed by an airman at RAF Sculthorpe. The RB-45 was also based in Britain and was used by the Royal Air Force for clandestine operations over the Soviet Union. At least three surveillance missions were carried out. The B-45 "Backbreaker" was Grand Slam and nuclear capable.

However, by early 1948, the developing Cold War made the military threat much closer and more menacing. A Communist regime was established in Czechoslovakia in February 1948. In June of the same year, the Soviet blockade of Berlin began and lasted almost a year. As a result, in that year, Britain allowed the B-29 Superfortress to be based in East Anglia. These were nuclear capable. At the invitation of British Prime Minister Clement Attlee, on July 17th -18th 1948, some sixty United States Air Force B-29 strategic bombers landed at three British air bases on a thirty-day training deployment. For the first time, the U.S. Air Force had stationed combat aircraft in another sovereign nation during peacetime. Unlike the situation in Germany, where the United States had acquired its bases by right of occupation, the United States had no bases of its own in the United Kingdom. Moreover, the two nations had no formal agreement allowing this deployment. Six squadrons of strategic bombers constituted a sizeable military force to be deployed on British soil in peacetime, without formal agreements between the host nation and visiting forces. On November 13th 1948, the Air Ministry advised Washington that long-term use of stations by the USAF "was assumed." Thus, less than four months after the arrival of a thirty-day deployed task force, the governments of the United States and the United Kingdom had agreed that the basing of U.S. armed forces in the United Kingdom would continue indefinitely. On September 3rd to the 5th 1948, the B-29s participated in a British defence exercise, “Operation Dagger.” The B-29s were based at Marham, Lakenheath and Sculthorpe. These bases were felt to be not so secure and more vulnerable to attack. An emergency plan, called “Double Quick”, provided for the movement of B-29s to other areas of Britain, preferably the Midlands, which were less vulnerable to attack. “Double Quick” required four bases suitable for B-29 combat operations. Four airfields were procured: - Brize Norton, Fairford, Upper Heyford and Greenham Common.

Two events in 1949 which strengthened the US-UK partnership in the Cold War were the signing of the North Atlantic Treaty in April and the ABC (American, British and Canadian) Conference held in Washington during September. This was the beginning of the formation of NATO. At the ABC conference, officials agreed that the

RAF would oversee the air defence of Great Britain, while the USAF would increase the number of wartime bomber units operating from U.K. bases. The explosion of the first nuclear device by the Soviet Union in August 1949 left no doubt that there was an incentive for greater US-U.K. partnership in defence. As an additional sign of the co-operative efforts of the two air forces, the RAF agreed to commit fighters to the defence of the USAF bases, give radar coverage for the areas surrounding the East Anglian bases and furnish RAF Regiment forces to guard them. By 1951, nine bases, Bassingbourne, Lakenheath, Lindholme, Manston, Marham, Mildenhall, Sculthorpe, Wyton and Waddington were operational. As soon as they were activated, six more bases, Brize Norton, Upper Heyford, Fairford, Greenham Common, Woodbridge and Carnaby were added to the American inventory. The three-year Korean War broke out in June 1950 and in September 1950 the Labour government undertook a general rearmament programme.

The same day that the Attlee government commenced the nuclear programme on the 8th January 1947, the Ministry of Supply sent out letters to the aircraft industry, inviting them to submit tenders, under specification B.35/46, for a new bomber – an invitation which resulted in brilliant responses with revolutionary designs, particularly from Avro and Handley Page.

After the Second World War, the Royal Air Force was left with a fleet of obsolete bombers, such as the Avro Lancaster and the Avro Lincoln. Of all the services, the Royal Air Force received the most draconian post-war cuts, from a front line strength of 1500 bombers, down to 150. This led to acquisition of the first British jet bomber, the English Electric Canberra.

The English Electric Canberra was built to specification B 3/45, as issued by the British Ministry of Supply in 1945. It was Britain's first jet bomber and was actually conceived in 1944 by W. E. W. "Teddy" Petter, who later designed the English Electric Lightning interceptor and the Folland Gnat fighter/trainer. On the 7th January 1946 the contract was placed by the Ministry of Supply for four prototype aircraft powered by the Rolls-Royce Avon, with the proviso that one be powered by the Rolls-Royce Nene.

The Avro Lincoln, workhorse of the Royal Air Force, used operationally in Kenya and Malaya. Bottom right is an example used by the Empire Test Pilot's School (ETPS)

VX185 started life as a Canberra PR3 and was converted to a B (I) 8 in 1954

Canberra bombers in squadron service. The stripes were for the Suez operation of 1956

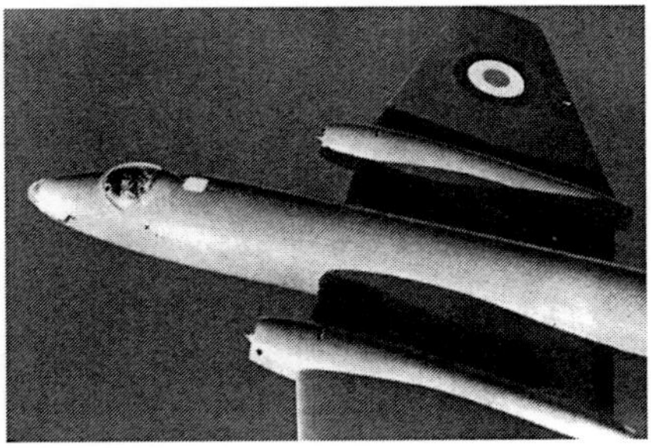

English Electric Canberra at altitude

The first two-seat prototype of the English Electric Canberra was flown in May 1949 at Warton airfield and in September it was revealed to the aeronautical world at the Farnborough Air Display. The aircraft, like the several variants subsequently developed from its basic design, demonstrated superior characteristics; not only could the new bomber take off and land in combat configuration on short and easily constructed runways, but it manoeuvred well at low and high speeds. The B.2, in contrast to the prototype, carried a crew of three, a pilot, navigator/plotter and observer. First delivery of a Canberra B.2 was made by Roland Beamont on 25th May 1951, when the type began to replace the Lincolns of 101 Squadron at Binbrook, Lincolnshire. Between August and December, the squadron was made up to strength with ten Canberras and a full complement of crews. Lincolns were subsequently replaced by Canberras in Nos. 9, 12, 50, 57, 61, 100, 199 and 617 Squadrons. They replaced the Washingtons of Nos. 15, 35, 44, 90, 115, 149 and 207, Mosquitos of Nos. 109 and 130 and Venoms of Nos. 6, 32, 45, 73 and 249. Newly-formed Canberra squadrons included Nos. 10, 18, 21, 27, 40, 59, 102, 103and 104 and B.2s were also supplied to Nos. 51 and 98 Squadrons of Signals Command for calibration duties. The second Canberra squadron to form was No. 617, the "Dam Busters", receiving its aircraft in January 1952. Altogether, five squadrons received Canberras that year, ten in 1953 and eight more in 1954. The Canberra went on to become a reconnaissance/ELINT/ trainer and was widely exported.

Avro 707 flying scale Vulcan models

Avro Vulcan XA891, development aircraft, lost 24th July 1959

Avro Vulcan XA897, the first Vulcan delivered to the Royal Air Force

AVRO VULCAN
now in squadron service with the R.A.F.
The Avro Vulcan, the world's first 4-jet delta bomber, has entered the Royal Air Force for full squadron service. Behind the recent Air Ministry announcement lies a brilliant chapter of aeronautical progress that marks the beginning of a new era in Britain's air power. With its near sonic speed, its great range and altitude and its large carrying capacity, the Vulcan can deliver a bigger bomb load faster, higher and further than any other aircraft. Add to this its fighter-like manœuvrability, exceptional safety and pleasant handling characteristics and you have the reasons why the Vulcan is the most effective bomber in service today. But that is not all . . . the Vulcan has a great development potential . . . it has been engineered to allow for new operational requirements which can be met without major alteration to the basic design. In the tough testing ground of the R.A.F. on routine exercises and on long-range training flights, the Vulcan is already showing its paces. Like its illustrious predecessors from the Avro stable – the Lincoln, the Lancaster, the Anson, the 504 and many others – the Vulcan is destined to become one of the world's really great aircraft.
A. V. ROE & CO. LIMITED — MANCHESTER / ENGLAND
Member of The Hawker Siddeley Group / Pioneer...and World Leader in Aviation
AVRO

A formation of Vulcans

XA890 shows the Vulcan's outstanding fighter manoeuvrability. This was the second production Vulcan B.1, retained for trials, before being scrapped in 1973

The first "V" Bomber to be ordered was the Avro Vulcan. The designer of the Vulcan was Roy Chadwick, who opted for a delta wing configuration, as found on some of the early German jets. To test the delta concept, a series of piloted flying models was built. The first model, the Avro 707, flew on 4th September 1949. Piloted by S. E. "Red" Esler, the Avro 707 was powered by the Rolls-Royce Derwent engine and demonstrated at the Farnborough Air Display. A year later, the Avro 707B was flown, piloted by R. Falk. It, too, was demonstrated at Farnborough that year and was very much a pilot's aeroplane. Unfortunately, it had problems with turbulence around the air intakes and cockpit. Modifications to the airframe were carried out on the third flying model, the Avro 707A. A second Avro 707A joined the test programme in 1953, followed by the side-by-side, two-seater, the Avro 707C. In total, five small Avro 707 delta wing research aircraft were built. They were, in effect, one third scale models of the Vulcan. They gave valuable data on the Vulcan's probable flight characteristics and were involved in trials at Farnborough and R.A.E. Bedford.

The Avro tender for the Avro 698, the Vulcan, was accepted on November 27th 1947. Of all-metal, stressed skin construction, the wing was some 7ft. thick at the root-end, enabling drag to be kept to a minimum, by enclosing engines, undercarriage and fuel and bomb cell entirely within. The Vulcan had been designed around the Bristol B.E.10 (Olympus) two-spool turbojet, but none was available for the first prototype. As a result, when it flew for the first time on 30th August 1952, piloted by Roly Falk, it was powered by four 6,500 lb.s.t. Rolls-Royce Avon, R.A.3s. In trials at Boscombe Down, the Vulcan showed that it required wing modifications. The Boscombe Down trials showed that application of "g" at altitude could initiate buffeting, which could lead to fatigue failure of the outer wings. In October 1955, the second prototype, VX777, was flown with leading edge sweepback reduced from 52 to 42 degrees at half span, but increased further outboard. This modification took away Chadwick's pure delta wing configuration.

The Avro Vulcan completed its acceptance trials during the spring of 1956 and the Vulcan BMk.I then entered service with No. 230

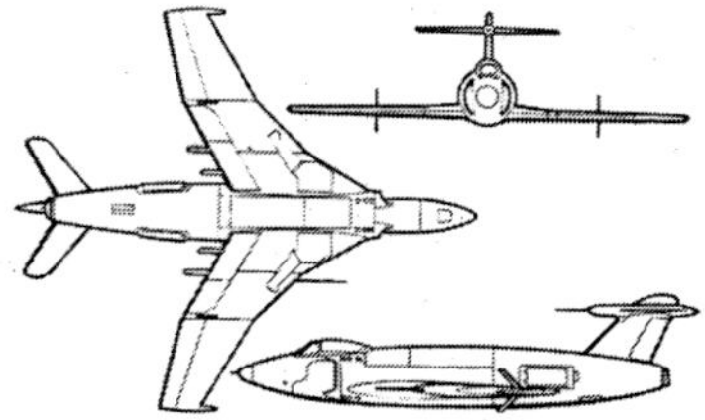

The HP 88

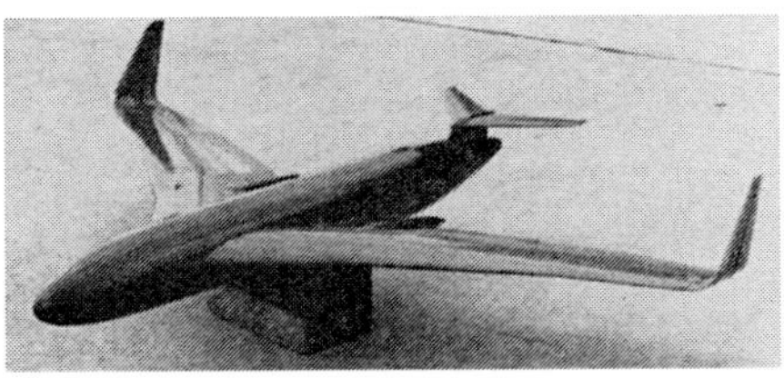

Early wind tunnel model of a Victor

The first Victor prototype WB771

FASTEST FARTHEST HIGHEST
V for VICTOR
Surpassing the most stringent operational requirements, the four-jet crescent-winged Victor is Britain's premier bomber.
V. 12
HANDLEY PAGE · RADLETT · LONDON · READING

Victor B.1 in Royal Air Force service, showing its elegant lines

The Handley Page Victor in Royal Air Force service

Operational Conversion Unit, at Waddington, on 22nd February 1957. 83 Squadron, the first operational Vulcan unit, was also formed at Waddington, on 11th July 1957. It was joined, subsequently, by Nos. 101 and 617 Squadrons. The planned re-equipment of three Bomber Command squadrons with the Mk.1 version was completed by the beginning of 1960. The B2 version was designed for Skybolt and Blue Steel and was powered by a more powerful Bristol Olympus. It won its combat laurels in the evening of its life, during the Falkland's War. It also flew as a strategic maritime reconnaissance aircraft and ended its service life as a tanker.

The second V Bomber to be ordered was the Handley Page Victor which was produced to specification B35/46. The Victor was designed to the same general requirement as the Avro Vulcan and was capable of carrying heavy loads at high sub-sonic speeds for great distances, at altitudes well over 50,000ft. As with the Vulcan, Handley Page commenced trials with a flying model of the aircraft's characteristics. The model, known as the HP88, was built by Blackburn around the fuselage of a Supermarine 510. First flown on the 21st June 1951 at Brough, the model proved the concept of the H.P.80, the Handley Page Victor. After flying for about 40 flights and with less than twenty hours flying time, the H.P.88 broke up over Stansted, killing the pilot. It had been flying for about 14 minutes when it suddenly broke up in the air. Witnesses said that they heard a strange engine noise, the aircraft started to fly vertically, flew upside down and then broke up over the runway, with burning wreckage landing on the tarmac. The cause of the accident was never determined.

With two prototypes being ordered on 26th April 1948, production of the Victor got underway, despite the loss of the HP88. The prototype Victor (WB771) first flew on 24th December 1952 and the second prototype (WB775) on 11th September 1954. The Victor was powered by four Armstrong Siddeley Sapphire axial flow turbojets which were based on the earlier Metropolitan Vickers design, the Metrovick F.9

The first production Victor (XA917) made its maiden flight on 1st

Prototype Vickers Valiant, with narrow air intakes

2nd prototype, with larger air intakes

In squadron service

Working on a Valiant tail

XD823 in anti-flash white

Valiant XD823 at altitude.

Valiant XD827 was used on the Grapple "Z" trial, 1958

49 Squadron Valiant WZ366 dropped Britain's first atomic weapon, at Maralinga, during "Operation Buffalo"

XD822

February 1956. It differed from the prototypes in having the nose lengthened by over three feet, to improve the C.G. and a reduction in the height of the fin. The first Victor B.1s to enter RAF service were delivered to No. 232 O.C.U. at Gaydon on the 28th Nov 1957. The first operational squadrons equipped with the Victor bomber were numbers 10 and 15 at Cottesmore.

About 50 Victor B.1s were supplied to the RAF, the last being XH 667 delivered in February 1961. Provision for in-flight refuelling and under-wing fuel tanks (first flown on XA930) became standard. The Mk2 version was powered by Rolls-Royce Conways. The Victor became a tanker, replacing the Vickers Valiant in 1965- 66. It, too, won its laurels in the Falklands War as a tanker. It was also used as a tanker in the first Gulf War. The Victor never dropped a bomb in anger.

The third V bomber to be ordered was the Vickers Valiant and the first to enter service. From 1955, Valiants began to arrive in Bomber Command.

The Vickers Valiant was designed around the Royal Air Force bomber requirement of 1947, for an advanced design for a jet bomber with wings of some 35 degrees sweep-back. The Valiant was seen as an insurance against the delay of the more advanced V Bombers.

The next year, 1948, Air Ministry Specification B.9/48 was drawn up around the Vickers design, which was allocated the Vickers Type number 660. The prototypes were ordered by contract on 2nd February 1949, the first to have four Rolls-Royce Avon R.A.3 turbo-jet engines and the second prototype, as Type 667, to be powered by four Armstrong Siddeley Sapphire turbojets.

Design commenced in 1949 and in 1950, components were being made into complete assemblies at Foxwarren. Although the bomber was ordered "straight off the drawing board", prototypes were still required at the time. As the Valiant, (as the B.9/48 bomber was subsequently named), it was to become Bomber Command's first four jet, swept wing bomber. Final assembly of the Valiant began early in 1951 at Wisley and the first flight was made by J. "Mutt" Summers, accompanied by G. R. "Jock" Bryce, from the grass airfield there on 18th May 1951.

Early flight trials of WB2I0 had given sufficient indication of the promise of the design. The second Valiant, WB2I5, flew on 11th April 1952, also at Wisley, with R.A.7 Avons and not with Sapphires as had been originally planned.

The first Squadron to receive the Valiant was 138 at Gaydon, Warwickshire, on 1st January 1955. 232 Operational Conversion Unit (OCU) was also formed there on 21st February 1955, to train V Force personnel in the operation and maintenance of the Valiant. The principal stations which operated the Valiant were, Marham, Honington, Wyton (reconnaissance) and Gaydon (OCU).

During October 1956, Nos. 138, 148, 207and 214 Squadrons moved to Luqa, Malta, from which base their Valiants went into action in the Suez campaign, becoming the first of the V Force to drop their bombs in anger.

The Valiant had been selected as the first, dedicated airborne tanker, but was prematurely withdrawn from service in 1965, due to failure of the wing-spar attachment castings, which had been manufactured from an unstable and poorly understood aluminium alloy material, DTD683. A kit was designed to fix this fault, but proved to be impractical to install and was abandoned. Only one complete Valiant survives to this day, in the Royal Air Force Museum.

Attempting to fill the gap between the time that the Avro Lincoln became hopelessly obsolete and the new V-Bombers entered service, the Air Staff issued specification B.14/46. This was for a less sophisticated, interim bomber, the Short S.A.4 Sperrin, powered by Rolls – Royce Avons. This was expected to enter service if any of the V bombers failed to go into production. Thus, in 1948, the financially strained U.K. found its aircraft industry committed to the development of five jet bombers. Mindful of its experience with Stirling, Halifax and Manchester bomber development, prior to World War II, the RAF balked at channelling all its efforts into one four-engine bomber design, for fear that it might make the wrong decision. Fortunately, the establishment of the Mutual Defense Assistance Program, by the U.S. Congress in 1949, provided the RAF with the opportunity to bypass production of the expensive Sperrin and

Short Sperrin used for high altitude bomb sight trials

VX161 on display and in the air

Sperrin being used as a Gyron test-bed

acquire, the production less capable, but "free" B-29s, for use as an interim bomber. Apparently, satisfactory progress on the Canberra and Valiant, coupled with the prospect of acquiring the B-29s from the U.S., mitigated the need to produce the Sperrin. The S.A.4 programme continued as a research project and Short eventually built two test aircraft, while B-29s and Canberras filled the interim bomber role. These two Sperrins were used to develop high altitude bomb sights and weapon devices (second prototype VX161) for the V bombers and as a test-bed for the de Havilland Gyron jet engine.

They RAF never intended the B-29, named Washington B.1 in British service, to fill its long-term need for a strategic bomber, but it gave the service that capacity. The B-29s were intended only to bridge the bomber gap, until domestically produced jet bombers became available and were received from March 1950. Acquisition of the eighty nine (plus 71 allocated as spares) B-29s enabled Bomber Command to maintain a strategic bombing capacity, saving the British taxpayer tens of millions of pounds and freed up the engineering and production capacity that would have been consumed by further Sperrin production.

Could the Washington have been used to deliver a nuclear device? In all probability, "Yes". There were five British devices available during the period of its service.

The Royal Air Force was unhappy at deploying the Washington, because air and ground crews had to be trained and resources set aside for its deployment. It was also a very expensive aeroplane to operate and the engines needed constant monitoring (90hrs between overhauls), as did the airframe. Reflecting the manpower crisis of the time, the Washington often flew without its full complement of gunners. Many Washingtons were placed in open storage at the Prestwick factory of Scottish Aviation, because there was no available storage space at the Maintenance Units. Scottish Aviation had been chosen as the civilian contractor for the Boeing Washington B.1. The Washington remained in service until 1958, with the last being used for clandestine, ELINT operations in the Eastern Mediterranean and the Baltic.

Tested to destruction at Foulness Island, during Blue Jay and Red Dean tests, such was the end for Washington WF436 in 1957

Preparing the B-29 test wing

The tower contained the Red Dean charges

B-29 bomb bay and fuselage under test

Washington B.1 in Royal Air Force squadron service. In the event of war they would be reassigned to Strategic Air Command

Washington B.1 on return to the United States, serial painted out. In 1950 atomic bomb casings were delivered to the U.K. for the British B-29s, the nuclear capsules remaining in the U.S.

Boeing Washington B.1 in open storage before being scrapped. In some cases, the Washingtons carried two serials in RAF service with no serials beneath the wings

Boeing Washington B.1 WW346 at El Adem in July 1956, part of a formation of four en route to Aden, from Marham. They flew in formation over Egypt and Cairo to Aden and also on the return flight.

Nose view of a Washington B.1 on the return flight to the U.S.A. The upper turret has four Brownings

Viewed from the cockpit – sleeves rolled up

Royal Air Force Washington B.1

Some of the airframes were not returned to the United States, being destroyed in explosive trials for missile warheads (Red Dean and Blue Jay) at Foulness Island in the late 1950s.

President Dwight D. Eisenhower and Prime Minister Harold MacMillan at their Bermuda Conference in March 1957, re-confirmed Anglo-American co-operation, although Eisenhower was hopping mad at the UK for the Suez operation in 1956 and the United States' inability to penetrate British codes and signals traffic at the time. There were also successful Anglo-American negotiations over nuclear information and materials and the deployment of the Thor IRBM. The complicated technical and financial agreement, the training of personnel to operate the weapon and the actual deployment and emplacement of sixty missiles were extraordinary achievements, but in one significant respect, the programme came up against an immovable obstacle - Blue Streak, the British IRBM, was in trouble.

In June 1959, the British Nuclear Deterrent Study Group was formed to look at Blue Streak's vulnerability to a pre-emptive strike. It could have credibility only as a first-strike weapon, costs were over-running and its deployment was unattainable, so it was abandoned in early 1960. Britain then agreed to accept Thor for four squadrons (60 operational missiles), which would be manned by Royal Air Force personnel, with the United States retaining custody of the nuclear warheads. In 1958, 70 Squadron at Feltwell, was first to receive the missiles, where they were stored horizontally in containers, the remaining units becoming active in 1959. All units had disbanded by 1963.

Blue Streak

Thor

Flying Officer Mills, RAF Thor Liaison Officer

Esprit de Corps
The Royal Air Force and Blue Steel

In 1947, the Long Range Weapons Establishment (LRWE) of which the Woomera range in Australia was a part, was set up. At the same time, negotiations with America on atomic co-operation had broken down, with the arrest of Klaus Fuchs and the perceived concept that the security of British atomic projects had been compromised and breached. Any request by Britain for use of the Nevada test ranges for atomic experiments was always met with a single answer, "No!"

With no access to American test sites, Britain had to look abroad for other test locations. At Woomera, in Australia, ample open test sites were available for Britain's use. The Australian Prime Minister, Sir Robert Menzies, quickly agreed enthusiastically to the British proposal that the Australian Monte Bello Islands also be used. As these decisions were being made, there came an unexpected proposal from the United States and Dr Penney was sent to follow up the offer. The Americans had proposed the Nevada site and also a Pacific site for Britain to test her first atomic bombs, but there was a catch. The Americans wanted all details of the weapon, plus drawings and of course Dr Penney was instructed to say, "No!"

By January 1951, a report had been prepared on the use of the Australian Monte Bello islands for atomic bomb experiments. This was to be known as "Operation Hurricane."

The design, planning and manufacturing expertise of British nuclear weapons was carried out at Fort Halstead, in Kent. The organisation which was set up there, for these and other explosive devices, was latterly called, "Armament Research and Development Establishment." This department arose out of two separate departments, the "Research Department" and the "Design Department", which were established in 1922. Before 1955, there was a department which operated under the name of High Explosive Research – "HER". The Chief Superintendent of Armament Research at this time was Doctor William Penney.

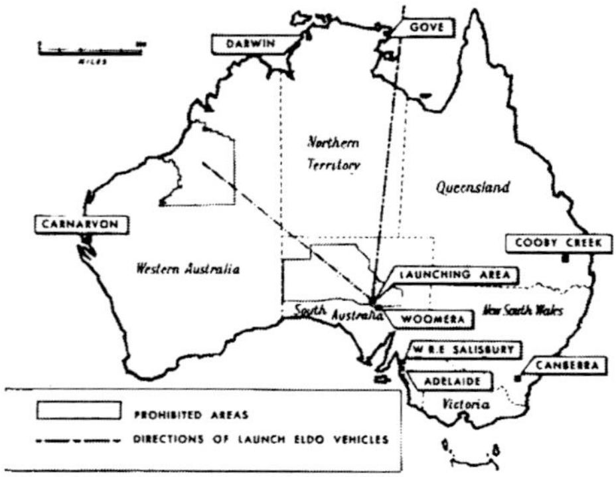

Australia - the testing areas

HMS Campania, former Festival of Britain ship "Campania" in 1951. She was command vessel for Operation Hurricane.

HMS Plym, the target vessel for Operation Hurricane.

Apart from the military considerations, British Civil Defence had concerns that security could be compromised by sending a ship, loaded with an atomic device, into the Port of London. The command vessel for this operation was the carrier vessel, HMS Campania (This vessel had previously been extensively fitted out for the Festival of Britain in 1951.). Two landing ships, HMS Zeebrugge and Narvik, were to transport a detachment of Royal Engineers and their heavy, civil engineering equipment. On arrival in the Monte Bellos, Zeebrugge was to act as a laboratory for the radio-chemists, while another landing ship, HMS Tracker, would be the health control vessel and health physics laboratory. A River Class frigate, H.M.S. Plym, which would transport the armed test weapon, was secretly designated as the target vessel. Destined to be destroyed in the explosion, Plym was to be fitted with an elaborately equipped weapons room, in which the device could be safely detonated by remote control.

Air transport for the operation was essential and this was by four Handley Page Hastings transport aircraft and Short Sunderland flying boats, which took the atomic materials to Monte Bello.

William Penney was in charge of the operation and was supported by ten RAF officers, led by Wing Commander J. S. Rowlands and other joint service staff, who were closely involved in the design of the weapon. Rowlands and his carefully selected team collaborated most successfully with the scientists. They also had an essential role in providing long-distance communications and transport. Dr Penney had asked that the assembly and loading of the fissile material should be done by the RAF.

By the time that the test was to take place, Winston Churchill had returned to office as Prime Minister. On 3rd October 1952, an atomic device, similar to the Fat Man bomb of 1945, was detonated inside the hull of H.M.S. Plym, vapourising the ship. With the test being a complete success, Churchill sent Australian Prime Minister Menzies and the people of Australia a message of thanks and a report of the operation and thanked the previous Attlee administration for starting Britain's nuclear programme.

The Short Sunderland flying boat flew at least three transport missions from Singapore, carrying fissile material and Dr Penney with others. To the left is a Royal New Zealand Air Force example.

Handley Page Hastings

Avro York transport used in Australia

The Bristol Freighter

The Douglas Dakota had two roles, that of transport and ocean surveillance

Penney and his team went on to produce an air-dropped, nuclear bomb, based on the Monte Bello "British Fat Man" of 1952. This was Blue Danube. Most of the casings were manufactured by Hudswell Clarke and Co. Ltd, Leeds, while Percival Aircraft, Luton, also played an important part in the design, which contained the high explosives and fissile components. Some of its internal electronic components were manufactured at HER, Fort Halstead, while other parts were produced by a number of private companies. Deliveries to the RAF had already begun in November 1953, but an operational test was obviously desirable as soon as possible, if only to give at least one aircrew the experience of dropping the device. Blue Danube was a very large bomb, being 24 feet long, 5 feet in diameter and weighing 10,000lb. In November 1953, the Air and Naval staffs issued an Operational Requirement, for a smaller weapon, OR 1127 (that is, smaller in size, not necessarily in yield), that could be carried by tactical aircraft, rather than the large, strategic bombers required for Blue Danube. This bomb, known as "Red Beard" was half the size of Blue Danube and weighed only a fifth as much. A much-sanitised version of Blue Danube was tested in the "Kite" series of bomb trials, when it was dropped by a Vickers Valiant. By early 1956, Red Beard had been included in British designs for the Green Granite thermo-nuclear warhead, testing of the primary warhead being of the utmost importance. There is evidence to suggest that the casings for Blue Danube were test-dropped at the Luce Bay Bombing Range in South West Scotland.

The eventual climax of the early British atomic bomb development occurred on 11th October 1956 when, in the Operation Buffalo trials at Maralinga, South Australia, a live Blue Danube was successfully dropped from a Valiant (WZ366) of No 49 Squadron, captained by Squadron Leader Edward Flavell.

Operation Grapple was formed to test nuclear weapons in the 400 megaton range, these being very early hydrogen bombs. The tests took place from 1956 to 1958 at Christmas Island on British possessions in the Pacific. Again, William Penney was in charge of the project. Britain was also interested in testing another two warheads, codenamed Short Granite and Purple Granite and another warhead, Orange Herald. The weapons system used to deliver these bombs was Yellow Sun.

An option was built into the programme named Green Bamboo. This was a megaton bomb of the concept known as Type A and used thermonuclear reactions to boost a large fission warhead. Green Bamboo was designated as a secondary weapon in the Grapple trials.

Orange Herald Large was another weapon designated for Grapple and was only to be used in dire emergency. This weapon never left British shores. A version of Short Granite, called Green Granite, was also considered for Grapple. A small warhead, codenamed Blue Fox, was one of the first warheads tested. This was a prototype warhead for a small surface-to-air guided missile (SAGW) and it was considered for the Bloodhound guided missile.

By May 1957, Britain had tested 21 nuclear devices. In comparison, the Americans had tested 67 at Bikini. Strangely, for a government that was committed to a nuclear programme and allocating billions into its production, the United Kingdom was unusually frugal (stingy) during the trials. One scientist declared that the success of the Hurricane operation was due to three or four Landing Craft Mechanised (LCMs) and the professionalism of the Services. But the pace was now being set for the dropping of air-launched hydrogen bombs.

Four Valiants were deployed from Wittering to Christmas Island:-

2nd March 1957- XD818: Wg Cdr. K. G. Hubbard and crew, plus Chief Tech W.Caple
3rd March 1957- XD822: Sq. Ldr D. Roberts and crew plus Chief Tech T. Small
4th March 1957- XD823: Sq. Ldr A. Steele and crew plus Chief Tech W. Quinlon
5th March 1957- XD824: Sq. Ldr B. Millett and crew plus Chief Tech C. Mathers

The route, as planned by Bomber Command was as follows:-
Wittering to Aldergrove in Northern Ireland for a top-up of fuel prior to the Atlantic crossing
Aldergrove to Goose Bay in Newfoundland

Goose Bay to Namao
Namao to Travis AFB in California
Travis to Honolulu
Honolulu to Christmas Island

The Valiants were painted white to reflect the extreme atomic heat, which could destroy the Redux process of the airframe bonding. Eight Valiants had been brought up to Grapple standard for the operation, with over 2000 modifications to the airframe. The first Valiant, XD818, arrived on the 12th March, flown by Hubbard. By 13th May the test operation was ready to commence. Two Blue Danube cases had arrived by Valiant aircraft for assembly and by the day of the test operation the nuclear device was loaded into its Blue Danube case. When they took off on 15th May 1957, there were two Valiants in the operation, XD818 and XD824, the latter to give the crews nuclear weapons experience. They were also followed by a Canberra aircraft.

When the device was dropped by XD818, Valiant XD824 went immediately into the "Farnborough Manoeuvre". Farnborough had devised a so-called escape manoeuvre – a maximum-rate turn at Mach .76, 60° of bank and pulling 1.7G for 40 seconds, which then set the aircraft tail-on to the blast overpressure wave within a few seconds before the explosion. This gave about nine miles of separation at the moment of burst. Two sampling aircraft flew through the cloud and within 24 hours samples had been flown back to Britain by a Canberra.

The second Grapple test, "Grapple X", took place in November 1957. The first store had not produced the expected yield and it was decided to repeat it as soon as possible in "X". In April 1958, 'Grapple Y' was successful, with another megaton test carried out visually, as before. During "Y" there were also some very interesting experiments carried out into blind bombing, under radar control. In September 1958, 'Grapple Z' carried out two further megaton air-drops. There were also two kiloton shots, suspended under tethered balloons, in those final days of the Grapple trials.

There was only one aircraft accident during the Grapple operation. A Canberra of 100 Squadron was lost over Canadian airspace, as it approached the Atlantic seaboard. The crew of two had pressed on without sleep or food for 24 hours and had apparently lost control of the aircraft in bad weather as it landed.

Though some of the experiments in these trials did not meet the expectations of the scientists, it did make Britain a nuclear player. XD818 was the first aircraft to drop a hydrogen bomb and it was recognised by the Americans that the British had something. This made both nations more co-operative and resulted in a better understanding of the hydrogen bomb's military potential. It also meant greater co-operation on the political front.

Although Britain had gone on to develop a practical mixed rocket-powered fighter aircraft, the Saunders Roe S.R.53, the 1957 Defence White Paper effectively destroyed Britain's research into rocket powered aircraft, when the S.R.53 was cancelled. The Air Ministry had envisaged that rocket defence and the manned bomber would be the order of the day in the Royal Air Force. After 1957, there was no role seen for the pure day defence fighter aircraft, but things were not as they seemed.

The Soviet Union had developed a four-engined, swept-wing, turbo-prop, strategic bomber, the Tupolev TU95, NATO code name "Bear". This aircraft, a development of the earlier TU4, which was a reverse-engineered copy of the American B-29 Superfortress, was nuclear-capable. During WW2, four American B-29s had force-landed in the Soviet Union. The Soviets impounded the aircraft, dismantled them and eventually, at Stalin's insistence, produced an almost identical copy of the American bomber. This became the Soviet Union's first strategic bomber and evolved into the TU95 Bear. The TU95 had the range and performance to attack continental targets outside the Soviet Union and thus, posed a true threat to the West.

From Peenemunde had come more information about German experiments with missiles in the V2 class being launched from submarines. The existence of the submarine missile launcher was to have a profound effect on the deployment of future nuclear missiles.

As early as October 1949, the Royal Air Force was showing a delta-winged aircraft called a "Launcher", releasing rocket missiles at targets outside enemy airspace. A defence study, undertaken in

Britain during this post - war period, was the combination of the Avro Vulcan delta-winged bomber, now termed the Launcher, with a new type of missile called, "a propelled controlled missile." The requirement for this missile was drawn up around OR1132 and was accepted by the Ministry of Supply, which had taken over aircraft procurement from the old wartime Ministry of Aircraft Production. The contract to develop this aircraft/missile combination was awarded to Avro and much of the technology of this weapon came from the experimental work of the Germans and Vickers. The Ministry of Supply believed that the first trials with the new "Standoff Bomb" could start some three years after the award of the contract, with the Vickers Valiant as the initial "mother" aircraft. By 1958, a 2/5 scale model of the bomb was being test dropped at the Aberporth range by a Valiant bomber. By then, the standoff bomb was being officially referred to as "Blue Steel", but it was not thought of as a guided missile by the contractors; Avro referred to it as their, "tail-first aeroplane". To them it was more of an aircraft than a missile.

Blue Steel became a joint government and industry project with a variety of contractors: - Elliot supplied the navigation system, de Havilland Engines the power supply, the R.A.E. the weapon and Avro the airframe with all the ancillary equipment. The rocket motor was developed by Armstrong Siddeley and it replaced the earlier de Havilland powerplant. Problems with the stainless steel fuselage and much of the associated systems meant a two year delay for the whole system going into operation with the Royal Air Force. The greatest technical problem, apart from fuselage flexing, was associated with the powerplant. Much of the heat from the electronics was absorbed by the missile structure and interfered with the fuel management and guidance systems. The way round heat seeping into the airframe of the missile was solved by Avro, who installed a refrigeration system which took heat away from the missile body, leaving the computers to work in normal temperatures.

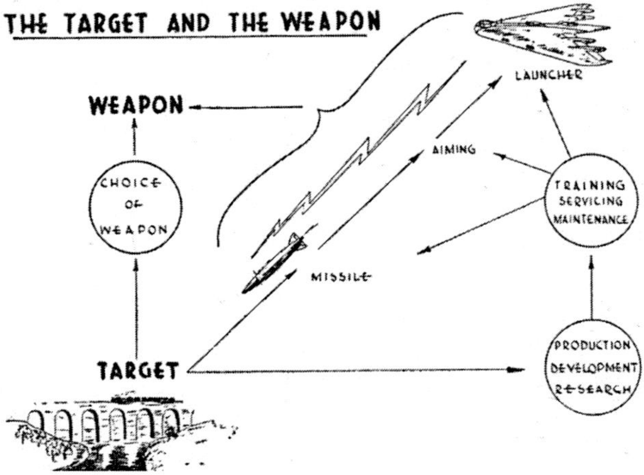

The 1949 genesis of the standoff bomb

Valiant WP204, used as a Blue Steel trials aircraft

Blue Steel deployed on Vulcan

AEC Blue Steel Transporter

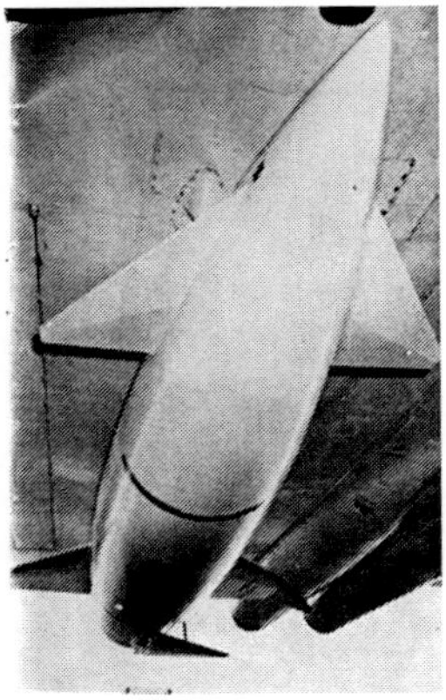

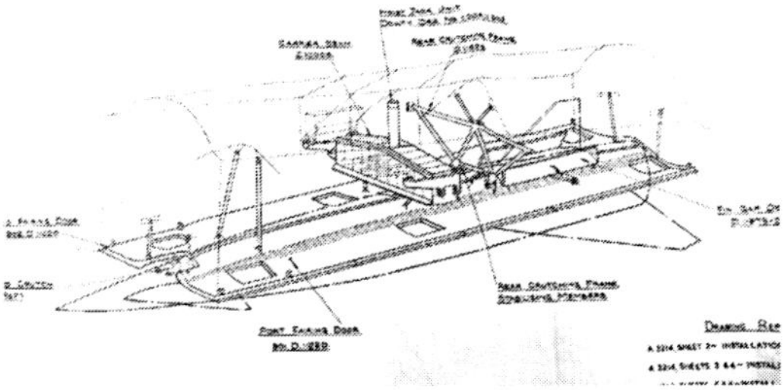

Blue Steel installed in a Vulcan and the Vulcan installation kit, MOD 200

AVRO BLUE STEEL

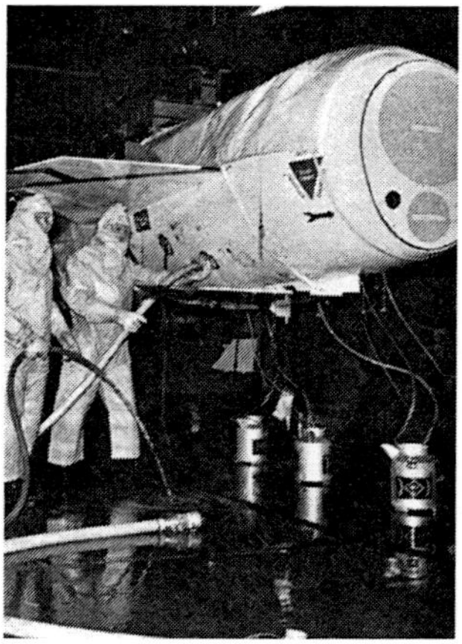

Operational Blue Steel missiles at Scampton with Vulcan XL361

A Handley Page Victor Mk2 carrying a Blue Steel

The date for the start of the whole Blue Steel programme is difficult to determine, but certainly the two major contractors, Avro and de Havilland and later Armstrong Siddeley, were working on the project as early as December 1953. The de Havilland rocket motor was designed for the early missiles by Edward Preece, while for Avro J.R. Ewens and P.L. Sutcliffe designed the missile. The missile had initially been designed with folding nose canards, which were in the retract position at low speed for launching. In the later, high Mach range, they were extended for high speed flight, but this feature was deleted in production models. On April 9th 1958 a "D" notice was issued to the British press restricting photographs of Blue Steel in a Vulcan to one image. By the end of 1958, two Valiants, WP199 and WP209 were dropping full scale Blue Steel models on the Aberporth Range and by 1960, successful live firing trials were being carried out in Australia at the Woomera test range. The smaller scale models of Blue Steel were built from light alloy, to be released over the test range, with the object of flight testing all the systems under operational conditions. These replicas were powered by a de Havilland Double Spectre rocket pack.

The Australian test phase was planned to take place between late 1957 and mid-1958. The aircraft involved in the test phase were:-

1. Valiant B.1 WZ370 mid-1957 to the end of 1958
2. Vulcan B.1 XA903 mid-1958 to the end of 1960
3. Valiant B.1 WP206 Dec 1958 to Dec 1959
4. Valiant B.1 WZ375 Mid 1959 to mid-1961
5. Victor B.1 Dec 1958 to mid-1960
6. Vulcan B.2 Jan 1960 to mid-1961
7. Victor B.2 mid-1960 to mid-1961

All aircraft were based and operated from Edinburgh Airfield. Preparations for the trials commenced in April 1956, with Avro starting work on the facilities. It had already been planned to use this airfield to test Red Dean, Blue Jay and Blue Sky. However, the Royal Australian Air Force was suspicious of a civilian contractor being used on such a secret operation.

Servicing the aircraft and supplying ground equipment was by Avro, while spares for the aircraft came through the Royal Australian Air Force.

Initial trials started with a 2/5 scale model which was planned to be launched between 1957 and 1958. A further 100 missile model launches were planned for 1958 to 1961, beginning with one drop per month, increasing to six by 1961.

Australia accepted the Blue Steel trials on 27th March 1956 and had agreed to finance the project facilities. Trials were to commence from January 1957, when a V bomber was allocated to the project. Blue Steel was to be regarded as an interim weapon, to fill the gap between a long range ballistic missile and a guided, ground-to-air weapon. The 2/5 scale model could reach 40000 feet and had a range of 50 miles, whereas the full scale model of Blue Steel had an altitude of 80000 feet and a range of over 150 miles.

The Blue Steel hypersonic standoff bomb/missile was 35ft in length, the foreplanes were 6ft 6in while the upper and lower tail fins were 13ft. Early versions of the missile were powered by the de Havilland Double Spectre (8000 lbs thrust), while the operational version used the Armstrong Siddeley Double Stentor (20000 lbs thrust), fuelled by two tons of hydrogen peroxide and kerosene. The weapon was officially in the 100 mile range, with an all up weight of nearly three tons. Blue Steel could be air-launched at 38000ft, climb to 59000ft at Mach 2.3, burn out at 80000ft and then dive onto its target, while the launch aircraft left the target area at sea level. The nuclear warhead was situated between the two, refrigerated fuel tanks. Interestingly, the Soviet intelligence service felt that the description of Blue Steel matched Bell Rascal and that both projects were linked.

The first Blue Steel training rounds were delivered to the Vulcan Wing at Scampton in the summer of 1962 and it was not until the autumn of 1964 that Blue steel was declared operational with all five Blue Steel squadrons. The first Vulcan squadron to be equipped with Blue Steel was 617 at Scampton and it took, on average, about fifteen hours to train a crew on the missile. The next two Vulcans squadrons to receive the weapon were 27 and 83.

With the proposed introduction of the TSR2 and Polaris, Blue Steel's operational role changed. As a result, the British government requested further facilities in Australia, from June 1963, to test Blue Steel in a low-level capacity. Blue Steel was planned to remain operational until at least December 1967, but events outside the control of the Ministry of Defence took an unusual turn.

TSR2

The Blue Steel Victor Mk2

Skybolt

The first American air-to-surface missiles (ASM), developed from German technology, were designed to give older U.S. bombers the ability to attack targets, without having to penetrate enemy air defences. This capability made the bomber more survivable at the cost of delivery accuracy. These early ASMs were also crude and in the case of the Rascal, difficult to use in time of war.

The Bell Rascal, built to contract W33-038 ac 14/69, was the first American strategic missile to be deployed on U.S. aircraft. The project proposal clearly stated that Rascal's prime warhead would be atomic. It was designed as an air-to-surface supersonic (Mach 1.6) guided missile. It was to be carried and launched from an altitude of 20,000 to 45,000 feet by a B-29 series aircraft, against stationary targets and manoeuvring water-borne targets at flight distances of up to 100 miles from the launching point. Using Rascal, the controlling aircraft had to be able to take evasive action in any direction, while controlling the missile and had to be able to execute control of the missile from a distance of at least 60 miles. Seventy-five percent hits within 500 feet of a stationary target and seventy-five percent direct hits on a water-borne target were required. The atomic warhead was designed to contain an explosive equivalent to at least 3000 pounds of TNT. Air Force plans called for three Rascal squadrons to be activated by late 1955, but stated a requirement for atomic warheads for only 34 percent of weapons.

Work started in 1946 on the development of a radar-relay guidance system. A simulated director and pilotless, parasite bomber combination, utilizing two B-17 aircraft, was equipped with an experimental Rascal guidance system. Reflecting the test results from this phase of the programme, an improved system for installation in a B-17/F-80 (simulating a director and missile combination) aircraft was also developed. This was, in fact, a progression of the German He111 carrying a V1 missile under the port wing. These were used late on in the Second World War to attack Britain from the North Sea.

First stand-off weapon, V-1 mounted on a Luftwaffe He111

B-17 with a JB-1, a copy of the V1

Bell Rascal

Rascal launched from a B-47

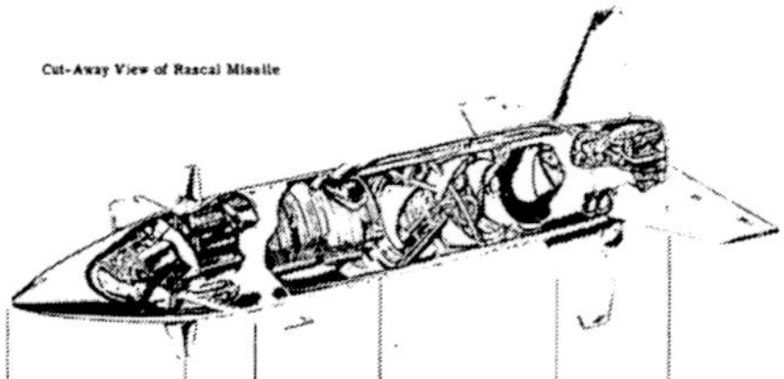

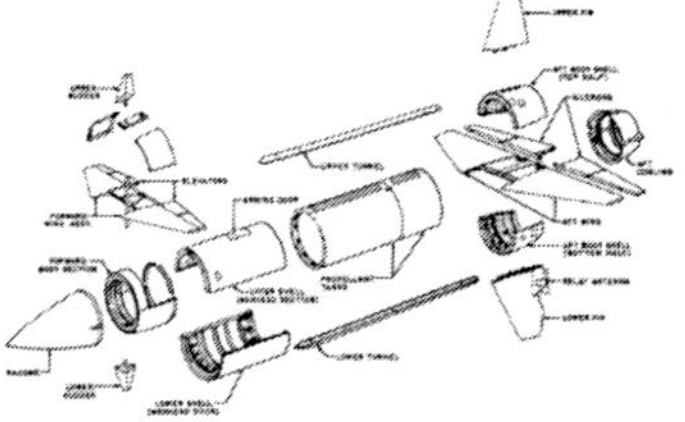

Bell Rascal cutaway drawing and equipment breakdown

Tests with B-17s and a version of the V-1, designated the JB-1, proved the concept of the air-launched missile and on the 29th April 1946, Bell Aircraft was issued with contract for a one year feasibility study of a subsonic air-to-surface missile. This contract marks the beginning of the Rascal programme. In May 1947, a second contract was issued, named Project MX-776, for the Rascal to be deployed by the B-29 Superfortress. The Rascal was a rocket-powered, supersonic, air-to-surface pilotless parasite bomber. Weighing 18500 pounds, it carried a 3000-pound warhead, at speeds in excess of Mach 1.0, with maximum in excess of Mach 2.0. It had a range of 90 nautical miles and an accuracy, based on a 75 nautical-mile range, such that 50 percent of the pilotless parasite bombers had an air burst strike within 1500 feet of a vertical line through the target and within plus or minus 405 feet msl of a predetermined altitude. Principal dimensions of the Rascal were as follows: - length, 32 feet diameter, 4 feet and a maximum horizontal span of 17 feet. A rocket power plant using white fuming nitric acid and gasoline propellants supplied 12000 pounds of thrust for a short period to accelerate the pilotless parasite bomber to supersonic velocity during its climb to altitude. For the remainder of the flight, a smaller, sustaining thrust of 4000 pounds was used to maintain supersonic speed.

In January 1948, Project MX-776 was divided into two concurrent programs:-

1. MX-776A (Shrike) - Design, development and fabrication was started on the Shrike missile, a supersonic Rascal test vehicle, with a 50 mile range and a load carrying capacity for warheads of up to 2000lbs. This was a 2/5 scale model of Rascal.
2. MX-776B (Rascal) – Work, initiated in 1946, on the development of a radar-relay guidance scheme for Rascal, was continued. By 1952 the Rascal had become the B-63.

With the second contract, Bell immediately went to work and on 28th April 1949, trials began on the first special test missile, the Shrike, to evaluate the aerodynamics and launching characteristics of the Rascal system. Though smaller than the planned Rascal and having only a 50 mile range, the Shrike tested the Rascal's aerodynamic design, radio control system, rocket engines and the bomber/launcher combination. In the spring of 1950, Air Materiel Command authorized Bell Aircraft to proceed with the detail designing and fabrication of the missile. The Rascal/Shrike programme was subsequently accelerated in August 1950 and in December 1951 the Air Force announced that the production Rascal would be designated the B-63. Early missiles were to be called XB-63s.

The first powered flight was completed on 30th September 1952 at Holloman AFB, White Sands, New Mexico and the first XB-63 pilotless parasite bomb, to fly under its own power, was released from a DB-50 director aircraft. In January 1953, the Shrike flight-test programme, which included 31 missiles, was successfully completed. The experience gained from this programme was now being applied to the XB-63. By the end of 1953, two glide and four powered XB-63s had been launched, the last having full guidance equipment. By 1958, the Rascal was termed "System 112A Rascal Weapons System". The lack of progress in testing the system was due to a shortage of trained personnel and inadequate availability of technical manuals. The two test areas were Eglin and Holloman Air Force bases and even by June 1958, the project was still not on track. At this stage, a Boeing B-47 was being used as the launch aircraft. The B-47, armed with a Rascal, could strike ground-based targets at a distance of 160 km, without entering into the air defence zone of the target. For transportation, the rocket was hung under the wing of the aircraft or on the right side of fuselage. The powerful, thick liquid propellant rocket engine, accelerated the rocket to one and a half times the speed of sound. Its guidance to the target was produced with the aid of the autonomous inertial guidance system, or radio commands from the carrier aircraft.

On 4th November 1954, the last B-29 bomber had been withdrawn from active service. This left only the B-36 and B-50 bombers as launching platforms for the Rascal. In June of the following year, the B-36 was also retired, the warhead requirements were revised and the inertial guidance system was deleted. Then, on 20th October 1955, the last B-50 bomber was retired, leaving the Rascal with only one

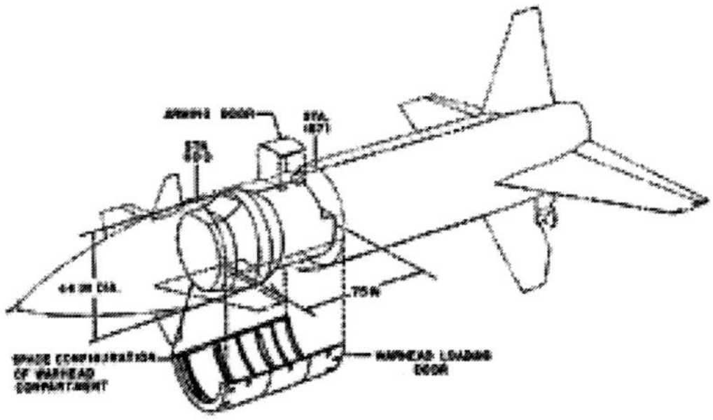

Rascal warhead location

Shrike, a scale model of Rascal, being readied for flight

A Shrike being launched from a B-50

launching platform, the B-47. Testing with this aircraft took two years and on 1st November 1957, the first Rascal /DB-47 unit, the 445th Bomber Squadron, was activated at Pinecastle AFB. The first all-SAC launch of a Rascal prototype occurred three months later, on 17th February 1958. By the time that the 445th BW had been activated, the Air Force had begun development of a new air-to-surface missile, Hound Dog.

Hound Dog was faster, smaller and more reliable than the Rascal. Since it used jet fuel, the Hound Dog was also easier to prepare for launch and could be kept in a ready-to-launch mode for long periods. To prepare the RASCAL for flight required special clothing and equipment. The fuels were also non-storeable, thus requiring the missile to be fuelled just before take-off. As a result of this on 29th November 1958, Headquarters U.S. Air Force ended the Rascal programme, in favour of the Hound Dog. The last Bell Rascal missile was withdrawn in 1959.

In February 1958, growing concern about both the perceived unfavourable shift in the strategic balance and the increasing vulnerability of penetrating bombers, prompted the USAF to accelerate the weapon that later came to be called the Hound Dog. (The name was lifted from a song by Elvis Presley.) The missile, first designated GAM-77, then AGM-28, initially flew in April 1959. North American built the Hound Dog with a canard, a delta wing configuration and an underslung J52 engine. The design requirements called for a 350 mile range and Mach 2 speed at over 55,000 feet. The AGM-28B carried a 1742 pound warhead (four megatons) 652 nm in a high level profile, 340 nm in a low-level (1,000 feet at Mach .83) profile. A B-52 could carry two of the inertially-guided missiles. North American delivered the first production Hound Dog in December 1959 and SAC launched its first AGM-28 in February 1960. By the following July, one wing was operational with the weapon, although the first airborne alert with it did not take place until January 1962. SAC crews soon found that they could shorten B-52 take-off rolls by using the Hound Dog engines in addition to the bomber's eight engines. (Bomber fuel could later be transferred to the missile.)

Hound Dog equipped the B-52 Stratofortress, from 1960 until 1975, retiring in 1978

Accuracy, while exceeding one mile at full range, was probably adequate, considering the four megaton warhead. But two other problems hindered the missile; reliability was a constant concern and in addition, the two five-ton missiles, carried on pylons, degraded B-52 performance. Nevertheless, the numbers of hound dogs in the B-52 fleet rapidly grew from 54 in 1960, rising to 230 the next year, 547 in 1962 and 593 in 1963. By August 1963, 29 SAC wings were operational with the AGM-28. Hound Dog production ended in March 1963 and the number of operational missiles declined in the late 1960s and early 1970s, to about 308 in 1976. The USAF phased out the Hound Dog in 1976, replacing it with the smaller (14 feet in length), faster (Mach 3) and lighter (2230 pounds) SRAM.

Britain's willingness and need, to rely on U.S. help was underlined when, in 1960, the British Government finally cancelled the Blue Streak ballistic missile project and announced, instead, that it would purchase the U.S. Skybolt air-to-surface missile, powered by a two-stage solid fuel rocket, for its V-bombers. Skybolt was developed by Douglas in 1959, to be a B-52-launched ballistic missile. To achieve greater penetration capability, Skybolt was to have been an early version of today's air-launched cruise missile or tactical air-to-surface missile (TASM), with sufficient range to provide a stand-off capability. It was originally planned that the Hound Dog would be replaced by AGM-87A Skybolt air-launched missiles and that a B-52 would carry four of these 1,000-mile-range missiles. By employing Hound Dog and later Skybolt, the manned bombers would be able to penetrate through increasingly difficult Soviet surface-to-air missile defences. Robert McNamara, the Secretary of Defense, concluded that a B-52 equipped with Skybolt missiles would be, “a more effective, efficient delivery system”. He also felt it to be a better option than the B-70, which was cancelled

The 1962 US Budget had not included additional development funding for Skybolt, in the belief that the 1961 appropriation could be stretched out. McNamara believed the project should either be terminated, or at least continued more cost effectively. Accordingly,

Advertising for the Douglas GAM 87 Skybolt

Vulcan B2 with Skybolt in the UK

Projected Victor with Skybolt

Vulcan with two Skybolts. Trials commenced in the spring of 1961 at R.A.E.West Freugh, Scotland

B-52 with four GAM Skybolts

a further $50 million was allocated for Skybolt development, in the revised 1962 budget. Arrangements were made in June 1960, to permit the British to participate in the development of this air-launched ballistic missile. It was also agreed that the British would be able to procure the developed missile for employment by Royal Air Force V-bombers. By fitting a British nuclear warhead to Skybolt, the Royal Air Force would be able to prolong the usefulness of its V bombers and the British would also have an independence of action that was not possible with the earlier Thor intermediate-range missiles, which had been jointly controlled by United States and British personnel.

"Skybolt was intended for the destruction of the important objects of the enemy by nuclear charges from a distance of 1600-2400 km from an altitude of 10500-13700 metres with a velocity of 960 km/h and reach in flight along the ballistic trajectory of the height/altitude of 320-480 km. The flight speed of rocket is more than 2 km/s. This rocket is made in the form of a two-stage flight vehicle. The overall length of "Skybolt" is 7.5 m in length of first stage 5.4m, the second - 2. 1 m. On the first stage there are/installed long fixed stabilizers. The second stage is equipped with the aero-dynamic controllers which are placed in the forward section On the B-52 bomber it can carry simultaneously two ballistic missiles.

After the engines starting on the carrier aircraft, the rocket will pass from the level flight to the climb with the subsequent ballistic trajectory flight. In target area the rocket will enter in the atmosphere at the relatively flat angle which must decrease heating its second step/stage. For the protection of the warhead from the superheating thick plastic materials is applied." – Machine translated Soviet Air Force technical/intelligence report on Skybolt.

The United Kingdom had intended developing the air-launched stand -off bomb as a Mark 2 Blue Steel, This would be powered by four Bristol Thor ramjets, two at each wingtip in the over-and-under configuration, a location made possible by their small size and light weight. With the availability of the Douglas Skybolt system from America, Britain decided to go American. Skybolt was intended for fitment into a later mark of Vulcan B2 and Victor B2 with strengthened wing points. There then came a series of decisions outwith

Britain's control. President Kennedy had decided to cancel Skybolt and adopt, as a nuclear deterrent, a submarine-launched missile system, named Polaris. (This system was heavily influenced by the earlier German submarine system found at Peenemunde.) Tests of Skybolt had begun in April 1962, but the first five tests had been failures. The first fully successful Skybolt flight occurred on 19th December 1962 when one Skybolt was launched from a B-52 and performed faultlessly. (The day that it was cancelled.) Douglas built over 1000 Skybolts.

This decision effectively negated any advance Britain had hoped to obtain with an air launched nuclear deterrent and at a meeting in the Bahamas, with the British Prime Minister, Harold MacMillan, President Kennedy allowed Britain to adopt the Polaris missile system. The go-ahead for Polaris meant that Blue Steel had to be continued operationally until Polaris was in Royal Navy service. In the light of tactical developments, Avro's Blue Steel was adapted for launching below 1000ft with the Victor and Vulcan force. In the summer of 1969, the Royal Air Force handed the nuclear deterrent role over to the Royal Navy. Even with the change in nuclear deterrence, the Royal Air Force was still flying Blue Steel on the Vulcan well into 1970, over a year after its role was transferred to the Navy.

As the Cold War thawed, Britain's nuclear capability consisted of a submarine force deploying the U.S. Polaris ballistic missile system, with a modified warhead and a stockpile of nuclear gravity bombs, called the WE177, primarily intended for delivery against land targets by a variety of aircraft. The need for WE177 grew out of a gap for the replacement of Yellow Sun by Skybolt and the introduction of Polaris. WE177 was the product of a joint Royal Navy and Royal Air Force requirement. Using a variety of delivery aircraft, trials were undertaken at RAE West Freugh in 1965. The principal test aircraft for the device was the Vickers-Supermarine Scimitar, using a parachute retarded store.

Royal Navy Scimitars of the type used in the WE177 weapon trials at West Freugh, Scotland. One is landing on a carrier. The other is carrying a WE177 pattern store on trials

A Buccaneer, similar to the WE177 trials aircraft.

The preliminary air trials were carried out with the aim of proving the operational reliability and safety of the system. The Llanbedr Meteor WH309 was also chosen for the trials and the equipment was built into the front of the port wing tip camera pod. The aircraft in the WE177 proving trials were the Scimitar XD229, Canberra WT309 and two Buccaneers. One of these Buccaneers, XK528, was tragically lost over the Luce Bay Bombing Range on 30th June 1966 when it exploded, with the loss of both crew members. The equipment in each case was similar, although the installation details varied. All rounds were treated as live and before loading were kept in a temperature-controlled environment. Delays in the system were caused by warhead modifications, but WE177 was with Bomber Command by October 1967. The order was completed in May 1967. Abroad, WE177 was allocated to the Canberra and later, the Vulcan Strike Wing at RAF Akrotiri, Cyprus and at RAF Tengah, Singapore. The weapon could also be used by a variety of carrier-borne aircraft.

Bomber Command merged with Fighter Command in 1968 forming Strike Command, and on 17th June 1969, HMS Resolution set sail from the Clyde Submarine Base, Faslane, on the Royal Navy's first Polaris Patrol. At midnight on 30th June 1969 the Royal Navy took over responsibility for the UK nuclear deterrent.

The development of the air-launched nuclear missile gave British industry, in the 1950s, experience in developing and producing brand new technology for the future. But it is one of those twists of fate that, because of treaty obligations early in the Twentieth Century, a whole series of weapons systems was designed, developed and produced, which was much more terrifying than those which were meant to be eliminated.

WE177

HMS Dreadnought, the first nuclear-powered British submarine

HMS Resolution, the first British Polaris submarine, shown commissioning in October 1967

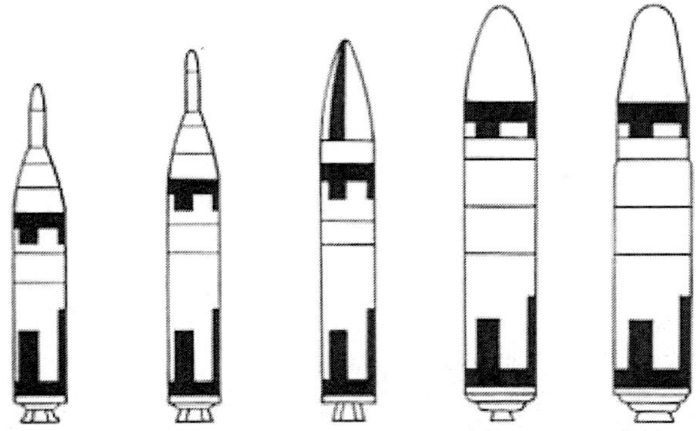

Submarine- launched ballistic missiles from 1960

Appendix

1. Inspection at Tarthum

2. Drones

3. Woomera

4. William Penney

5. Structure of the Royal Air Force 1970

6. V Bomber deployment

7. British Nuclear Testing

8. Silverplate

9. Avro Lancaster Nuclear Bomber

10. Personalities, Canberra etc.

11. The Quebec Agreement

Appendix 1

Inspection at Tarthum

"Research Aeroplane 8-346"

Date of inspection: 27 June 1945

Source: CIOS ER No149

RESEARCHER'S NOTE: *This document has not been conserved and it formed a small part of a major report but was damaged. The text was also difficult to make out or copy. The language would seem to suggest that the report was written by an individual whose first language was not English.*

DESCRIPTION*: The aeroplane is of all-metal construction (Duralumin) and propelled by two liquid –feed rockets. The semi-monocoque wing has an area of 216 square feet, a span of 30 feet and a large sweep back of 45 degrees. The spindle shaped fuselage is of semi-monocoque construction with a diameter of 5.2 feet. In the nose of it is the pilot's cabin, this is the pressure cabin for instruments of measuring. In the centre are the fuel tanks and further aft the driving gears, with the two thrust motors at the tail. These aggregates are known from the type 8-163, the tailless fighter. Also at the tail are fastened the tailplanes, which likewise have large sweepbacks. In the central part is furthermore built in a retractable skid for landing gear. All control surfaces are divided in two parts; the outer part of each has no aerodynamic balance (no nose part before the hinge) and a great proportion of the airfoil depth. So that in the supersonic range it shall remain efficient. (by protruding from the Mach angle).*

To avoid too sensitive control of the system direct, therefore alternatively one open or both parts of the control surfaces. The bottom of the pressure cabin the pilot lies upon can be catapulted and in an arbitrary altitude it will be automatically put off. The whole nose from the fuselage (the pilot's cabin) can be blown off by means of explosive bolts it is fastened with. A directional parachute will then reduce the dropping of the cabin. The pressure in this cabin will be regulated with an overpressure valve corresponding in altitude to 30000 feet. A supply of compressed air is stored on board and the pilots get oxygen for breathing. In every individual control system is built in a meter to

regulate the forces. The wing is fastened to the fuselage by means of measuring columns so that all the forces and moments of the wing in and about the three axis can be measured. The design is so laid out that with the addition of some tension metres on the supporting spar and by calibrating the last the locus of the centre of pressure of each wingside can be determined.
The forces in the columns and in the metres shall be electrically recorded with instruments in the special pressure cabin. All precautions are taken to make the ship for its task as safe as possible. The design load factor for the pull-out from a dive and for a reduced gross weight (reduced fuel supply) is 8 and therefor with a factor of safety of 1.8 the ultimate load factor will be 14.4.Also of great importance of furthermore is the safety against the flutter of the wing and the tailplane. Because all problems in the interesting range (and further for wings with large sweepbacks) are unknown. A.V.A. (Aerodynamishe Vershuchsanstaldt-Aerodynamic Research Institute) at Gottingen has been counselled and computing the dynamic (instationary) air forces and also the flutter velocities of this airplane for a variety of Mach numbers in the whole speed range.
TESTS: *At the beginning of the tests the flying qualities will be determined at a gliding flight of nearly V-900km/h (560 mph.) and then the airplane will be altered if necessary. At the tests the airplane will be carried by a carrier plane to an altitude of 10 km (33000 feet) and there started. If the flights are satisfactory the speed shall be gradually increased while the driving motors are switched on. For the final tests it is intended that the airplane will be started as usual at an altitude of 10 km (33000 feet) and then climb under its own power at an altitude of 20 km (66000 feet). (Since the thrust of ???????? the jets is larger than the gross weight a vertical climb is possible.) There it shall attain in level flight a speed of more than V-2000 km/h, 1650 mph. Then the flying qualities, especially the forces in the control column, will be measured and supporting forces of the wing on the fuselage and eventually the forces on the tailplane. We have reason to believe that the results of the planned tests will give us information unknown till now. Salient variations of the values and the working points of the air forces in the supersonic range and about the most unknown transition point. That will give us the possibility to determine in advance the flying qualities and the performances of high-speed airplanes, especially the automatically controlled planes in the same way as it is now possible in the usual speed range.*

SUMMING UP: *Research tests that give us information unknown till now, about the behaviour of air forces on airplanes in the supersonic range and about the transition point are of paramount importance for the design of super high-speed aircraft, as they will make it possible to avoid great errors with probably great consequences. Since the design of the research airplane 8-346 is very far in progress and the materials and driving gears (from the tailless fighter the 8-163) are at disposal and since at this time the men of the engineering staff are still accessible (before they are scattered) the building of this plane would be possible in a reasonably short time.*

Appendix 2

Drones

During and after the First World War there were many experiments with unmanned aircraft. These aircraft were to be gyro and radio-controlled aircraft, to be filled with bombs or explosives, or to be targets for anti-aircraft artillery. Britain was the pioneer in this field and kept the unmanned target aircraft programmes alive from the 1920s through to 1943. One of the first British models was a version of the Fairey IIIF reconnaissance float plane. Nicknamed the "Fairey Queen," it was used successfully in exercises against the Home Fleet in the Mediterranean, in January 1933.

The first mass-produced British model of a gunnery drone was named the "Queen Bee", which had a final production tally of 420, built from 1934 to 1943. This aircraft, designed by de Havilland, was wholly wooden throughout, with a wheeled undercarriage, which could be changed for floats. Scottish Aviation, one of the Queen Bee manufacturers, sub-contracted the work to the Scottish furniture industry.

The evolution of target drones started with the Queen Bee in the mid-1930s. In 1935, while attending the London Disarmament Conference, CNO Admiral William H. Standley, U.S. Navy, was provided with a demonstration of British aerial targets, including a Queen Bee. On 1st May 1936, after conferring with Rear Admiral Ernest J. King, the Chief of the Bureau of Aeronautics, he directed Rear Admiral Harold G. Bowen to proceed with the development of radio-controlled targets. On 20th July 1936, Lieutenant Commander Delmar S. Fahrney was put in charge of the radio-controlled aircraft project. In his semi-annual report for the last half of 1936, Fahrney introduced the term *drone* for radio-controlled aerial targets, a term used to this day. Work commenced on the airframe at the Naval Aircraft Factory in Philadelphia, while the radio equipment was developed by the Radio Division at the Naval Research Laboratory.

The Germans were the first to utilise a drone for attack in 1944, the V-1 rocket. It utilized a pulsing ramjet engine, an aneroid barometer, set to hold it at about 1,000 feet, a magnetic compass with a set heading, a gyroscope for stabilization and a propeller-driven device to measure air miles travelled, so it could command a dive into the terrain.

During the war, the United States also found an enterprising way to attack highly defended targets and dispose of B-17 Flying Fortresses that had flown out their useful lives. They stripped the bombers of all useful equipment, loaded them with up to 20000 pounds of explosives and modified the aircraft to be piloted via an open cockpit on the top of the fuselage. These were now designated the QB-17 and the programme was named, "Aphrodite". It was during Aphrodite, that Joseph Kennedy, brother of the future president of the United States, John F. Kennedy, lost his life in a drone B-24.

Another project, dubbed "Project Option," under the command of Commodore Oscar Smith, produced pilotless drones built by the Interstate Aircraft and Engineering Corporation, which were designated TDR-1. They were built with television guidance systems and controlled by a TBF Avenger. They could be armed with either a torpedo or a 2000-pound bomb.

Another American series of drones were the Culver PQ-14A and the Culver PQ8. They were built as target drones for the U.S. Army. The Culver Drone was usually controlled by a Beech C-45 or a Cessna UC-78 Bobcat, with many of them being shot down by army gunners.

The next real post-war stimulus to the development of target aircraft came with the production in Australia of the jet-engined Jindivik. Engine, autopilot and radio gear were produced in the U.K. Fireflies and Meteors were also developed for pilotless operation at R.A.E. Llanbedr for engagement by missiles launched from Aberporth. Target Meteors were also provided at Woomera and Canberras were converted by Short Bros, for use as target aircraft for missiles.

Queen Bee drone

Converted Queen Bee, Canal Zone 1954

A B-17 drone, controlled from Hawaii, shown flying to the west coast of the USA in 1945

Culver drone, with Cessna Bobcat

Interstate drone

Jindivik

Meteor

Canberra

Appendix 3

Woomera

A woomera is a wooden spear throwing device which makes the spear travel faster when thrown by the arm. The woomera has a hollow, curved section at the wide end and the other end is shaped like a hook. Apart from throwing a spear, the sharp end has other uses. As such, Woomera was the ideal name for the new rocket establishment.

Woomera is in South Australia, the closest major cities being Adelaide, Melbourne, Canberra and Wollongong. In 1946, Woomera was chosen as a joint Australian/United Kingdom Establishment for rocket testing. Building work commenced in 1947 and the site soon became the largest test area in the world for rockets. Initially, the cost was estimated at £12 million, but soared to £50 million. About four miles north of Woomera village, an airfield was built for the Royal Australian Air Force. This was used for test flying including Australian-built Mustangs and the Jindivik drone (at Evetts Field). Around November 1949, the first fourteen rockets were tested and in September 1952 two Boeing Washington bombers were allocated to Australia for test purposes. Although they were Royal Air Force aircraft, they were flown by Australian air crews and carried Australian markings. The crews were trained in Britain at an operational conversion unit. At least two Avro Lincolns carried out trials at the establishment, when Woomera was opened. In 1952 a Handley Page Hastings brought Dr Penney and Dr O.M. Solandt, a Canadian, to Woomera. Solandt was a "guided weapons expert" and nothing was revealed about this mission.

In 1953 it was agreed that all work carried out at Woomera by the Commonwealth of Australia would be paid for by the British government. By then Australia had spent A £30 million on the site.

Woomera became key to the atomic weapons trials at Monte Bello and about 80% of the equipment was flown from Woomera to the test area. The heavy ground moving equipment was transported by sea.

RAAF and RAF air crews and ground staff worked as a team within No. 34 (Communications) Squadron, RAAF, a wartime transport unit which had been reformed in March 1948 to operate the vital courier and transport services between Mallala, near Adelaide and Woomera. From Woomera to the Monte Bello Islands, the RAAF flew Bristol Freighters, owned by the Ministry of Supply (Aus.) and the RAF used the four-engined Avro York aircraft.

The first trial rocket launcher

An example of a G.A.F Lincoln

A crashed Mustang at Woomera

Rocket trials Meteor

A92-3, an early Jindivik from Woomera

Appendix 4

William G. Penney

William George Penney was born on 24th June 1909 in Gibraltar, where his father was stationed with the British army. He was a brilliant student at Imperial College, London and published his first paper at the age of 20. He worked with Ralph de Laer Kronig, partly in London, partly in Groningen, the Netherlands and together they developed the "Kronig-Penney model," a solveable model for the motion of electrons in periodic fields. After two years at the University of Wisconsin, under the renowned American quantum theoretician, John H. Van Vleck, who thought highly of him, on a Commonwealth Fund fellowship, he spent three years in Cambridge, collaborating with J. E. Leonard Jones, under whose influence Penney's interests turned from crystalline fields to molecules. Penney made many important contributions to theoretical chemistry while at Cambridge and he continued this work when he returned to Imperial College as an assistant professor. He was also a gifted sportsman.

On the outbreak of war in 1939, Penney started work for the British Admiralty on the structure and effect of blast waves on Mulberry Harbours and at the Home Office on the effects of high explosive. He joined "Tube Alloys" and became a British member of the Manhattan Project. This work led to his being invited in 1944 to Los Alamos. Soon after his arrival, he gave a talk about the effect of blast waves on people, including many gruesome details, to which his American audience was not accustomed. He presented all this with his usual, cheerful manner and so acquired for a time the soubriquet, "The Smiling Killer!" from the American physicist, Viki Weisskopf. He was one of the first scientists to visit the ruins of Nagasaki. After making notes and calculations, he estimated that the blast was equivalent to twenty-two kilotons of TNT, ten per cent higher than announced.

He impressed people at Los Alamos with his expertise and ability. As part of his close involvement with the Americans in the first peacetime nuclear tests on the Bikini Atoll in the Pacific, he was responsible for gauging the power of the blasts and the toxicity of the lingering radioactivity. He had some wooden boxes prepared with circular holes of various sizes, covered with paper. The blast would puncture the paper covering the larger holes, but not the smaller ones and by noting the size of the largest holes still intact, one could find the strength of the blast wave.

On his return to Britain after the war, he was appointed Chief Superintendent of Armaments Research at the Ministry of Supply. When the government, under Clement Attlee, decided to start developing nuclear weapons, Penney was put in charge. He was the only member of his group who had experience in nuclear weapons work. Since the US McMahon Act of 1946 prohibited exchange of information on nuclear matters, Penney, with his Los Alamos experiences, carried the sole responsibility for the development of the British A-bomb, a responsibility he discharged brilliantly. In a short time, Penney built up the Atomic Weapons Research Establishment at Aldermaston, which contained research and production facilities for making nuclear weapons. Leading this project required, not only scientific brilliance, but firmness of purpose and an ability to handle people. Penney proved to be an outstanding success in these respects – he was a natural leader and man-manager. Quiet and soft-spoken, patient and always cheerful, shunning publicity and with an exceptional ability to explain complicated matters clearly and simply, he became extremely popular with his staff.

The first atomic bomb produced by his team was successfully tested in 1952. It led, eventually, to a hydrogen bomb in 1957. For his work on this, Operation Hurricane, he received a knighthood. Penney was instrumental in restoring the exchange of nuclear technology between Britain and the USA in 1958, repairing "The Special Relationship" and he was credited with playing a leading part in the negotiations which led to the Test Ban Treaty in 1963. From 1954 to 1967, he served on the UKAEA Board, becoming Chairman in 1962. He served in that post until 1967, when he accepted an appointment as head of Imperial College. His open, informal manner gained him people's confidence also in the academic sphere and in 1968, when many universities had violent student unrest, Penney's influence preserved peace at Imperial College. He retired from Imperial College in 1973. He was created Baron Penney of East Hendred in 1967.

At hearings of an Australian Royal Commission in 1985, it was suggested that the health of Australian aboriginals had been damaged by British nuclear weapons tests. Though the allegation was not supported by the Commission, they chose to accept anecdotal evidence. Penney was deeply hurt, because he had taken great trouble to avoid any risks to the local population or the test staff by his methodical planning. He died on 3rd March 1991.

William G. Penney *(Los Alamos Image)*

Appendix 5

Structure of the Royal Air Force in 1970

RESTRICTED

ANNEX E TO AP 3365

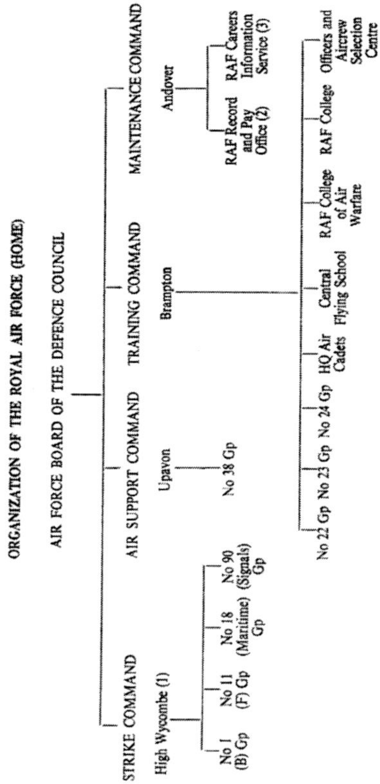

Notes:
1 Administrative Headquarters at Stanmore
2 Functionally controlled by DGM(RAF) and DGPS(RAF)
3 Functionally controlled by DGM(RAF)

(As at 1 Jan 71)

E–1 (AL 11, Dec 70)

RESTRICTED

ORGANIZATION OF A TYPICAL RAF FORMATION HEADQUARTERS

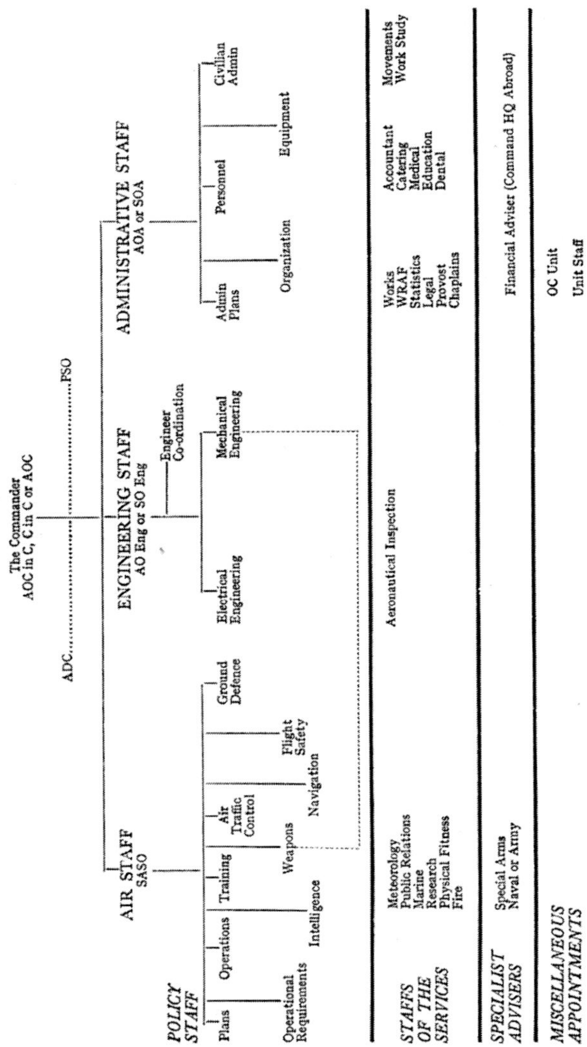

Note: Not all branches or services are represented at all headquarters, particularly at group level.

ORGANIZATION OF A TYPICAL OPERATIONAL STATION

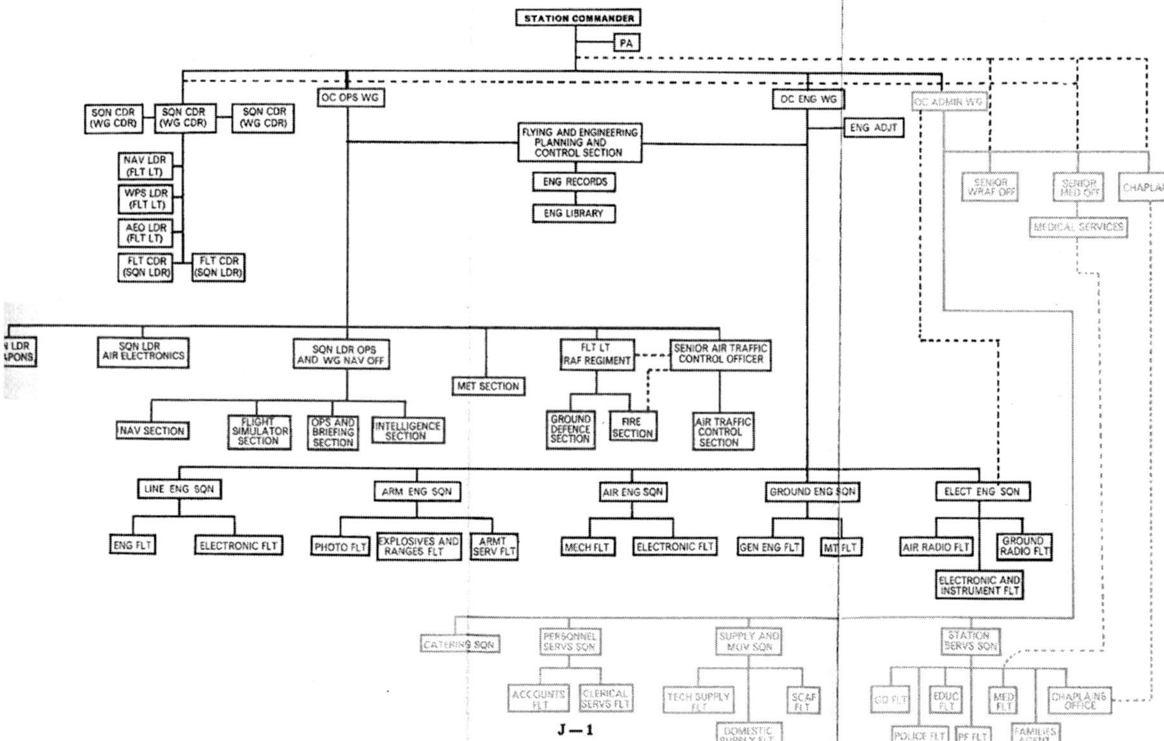

J—1

Appendix 6

V Bomber Deployment

Valiant Squadrons

138 Wittering, 543 Wyton (PR Role), 214 Marham, 49 Wittering, 207 Marham, 148 Marham, 7 Honington

Vulcan Squadrons

83 Waddington/Scampton, 102 Finningley, 617 Scampton, 44 Waddington, 27 Scampton, 50 Waddington, 9 Coningsby, Cottesmore, Akrotiri, Waddington, 12 Coningsby, 35 Coningsby, Cottesmore, Akrotiri, Scampton

Victor Squadrons

10 Cottesmore, 15 Cottesmore, 57 Honington/Marham, 55 Honington/Marham, 139 Wittering, 100 Wittering, 214 Marham

V Bombers and Canberras allocated nuclear stores

Canberra B (I) 8	1960 – 66	type----------
Canberra B. 15/16	1960 -	type----------
Valiant (MBF)	----------------	type----------
Valiant (TBF)	----------------	type----------
Vulcan B.1/1A	1963-	type----------
Vulcan B2	1963 – 19--	type----------
Victor B.1/1A	----------------	type---------
Victor B.2	1964 – 19--	type---------

Annexe A

Boeing Washington Squadrons

Boeing Washington B.1:- Nos. 15, 35, 44, 57, 90, 115, 149, 207, based at RAF Coningsby and RAF Marham within 3 Group. RB-29s also operated out of Watton with 192 Squadron and four were with Vickers for trials. RAF Maintenance Units: - 22MU, 23MU, 53MU and 58MU. Civilian support: - Scottish Aviation, Prestwick, Scotland. Two transferred to Australia for trials.

Appendix 7

British Nuclear Testing
Royal Air Force involvement

Operation Hurricane 1952
Operation Totem: 1953
Operation Mosaic: 1956
Operation Buffalo: 1956
Operation Grapple 1957
Grapple X/Round C 1957
Operation Antler 1957
Operation Grapple Y and Z 1958

Appendix 8

Silverplate

The modification of the Boeing B-29 Superfortress, to carry the first two atomic weapons was originally called "Silver Plated." The two weapons were "Thin Man" and "Fat Man." The code, "Silver Plated," was modified further to "Silverplate." It meant that the Pullman (Silverplate B-29) was to carry the President (Thin Man) and the Prime Minister (Fat Man) on a secret mission around the United States. On 1st December 1943, Silverplate B-29 modifications were given the highest priority. The first mission of the B-29 scheduled with the modifications was mid-February 1944.

The Silverplate modifications were entirely in the B-29 bomb bay and included the installation of a new H frame, C-6 hoist, sway braces, carrier assembly, antenna equipment, junction box, the British Type F release unit and type G shackle assembly and the Winkler type bomb bay doors installed. On 20th February 1944 the first Silverplate modified B-29 flew to Muroc Field and testing of the aerodynamic qualities of the bombs started on the 28th. By June 1944, for technical reasons, Thin Man became a uranium bomb and with that a change of name, to "Little Boy". By then the British bomb release gear had been adapted for the bombs. These tests confirmed that Silverplate worked and as a result, on the 23rd August 1944, the Glenn L. Martin Company, Nebraska, received the contract to modify the first three B-29s. Some more changes came about in January 1945 when the Americans produced a release and shackle much better-suited for atomic bombs than the British Type F and Type C gear.

In July 1944, the number of modified B-29s was increased from three to fourteen and on 22nd August 1944 to twenty five. By this time, added to the twenty four, was one which had been hand-modified by Wright Field. Apparently the hand-modified machine was to be kept as a permanent model.

In February 1945 the Air Force insisted that, instead of twenty four modified aircraft there should be forty eight, which with the Wright Field, hand modified example, made a total of forty nine. On 18th April the number was raised by five. Thus, when Silverplate was almost operational, it included fifty four B-29s, twenty nine of which had been modified in 1944 and twenty five of which were either being modified or were to be modified within the year. Only forty six were completed before the end of the war. For operations against Japan, fifteen Silverplate aircraft were assigned to Tinian.

In the first few months of peace, twenty two aircraft of the 509th Composite Group were placed in the Oklahoma City Air Materiel Depot for modification. An MX-344 radar computer and more easily-removed engine cowlings and performance improvement items were installed. Eight of these aircraft were assigned to Operation Crossroads and in February 1946, the number of Silverplate B-29s was increased to ten, but two were damaged beyond repair on the 6th March in a taxiing accident. Silverplate modifications were always under constant improvement and Air Materiel Command considered Silverplate modifications never finalised.

By April 1947, forty six B-29s had been modified and nineteen others in the process of modification, twenty were still being used by the 509th Composite Group, five of the aircraft had crashed, one had been seriously damaged in a fire, but was awaiting repair and one was being used as a mock-up for further standardizations of Silverplate. Four were at Kirtland Field, being used by the Flight Test Section and two were in the museum at Davis-Monthan. The remainder had been, or were being, stripped of their Silverplate equipment.

Due to the code word Silverplate being compromised, a new word, "Saddletree" was given to B-29s assigned to carry the atomic bomb. After May 1947, these B-29s could not be declared obsolete and were capable of carrying the stock-piled Fat Man. It was felt that, as late as September 1949, the Silverplate/Saddletree B-29s could still be used in an emergency, or to deploy atomic weapons overseas to forward bases. It was on 12th May 1947 that the name Silverplate was discontinued.

Modifications to the B-29s continued and another project was included, named "Chickenpox." This was an adaptation of the Boeing C-97 Stratofreighter, for use as flying assembly rooms for atomic weapons. It took 16 hours, using two crews, to prepare a device for transportation. Somewhat later, it was also suggested that the Chickenpox aircraft could be used, along with Silverplate B-29s, to transport the bombs from the United States to the forward areas in the ferry plan. At one point, it was even suggested that the C-97 could be used as a delivery system to a target. Thought was also to be given to the development of new atomic bomb-carrying aircraft and there was great interest in the use of guided missiles.

Forty-six B-29s had been modified as SILVERPLATE aircraft with location and serial number as indicated:-

1. Sixteen operational aircraft at Roswell Army Air Force Base

44-27298 "Full House"
41-27300 "Strange Cargo"
44-27301
44-27302 "Straight Flush"
44-27304 "Upan Atom"
44-27353 "Great Artiste"
41-27354 "Dave's Dream"
44-86291
44-86346 "Big Stick"
44-86347 "Laggin Draggin"
44-86382
44-86383
44-86364
44-86430
44-86432
44-87472

2. Two B-29s at Oklahoma City Materiel Command Depot.
44-27299 "Next Objective". Operational, awaiting delivery to SAC
44-86131 Awaiting storage and removal of Silverplate equipment

3. Five aircraft at Kirtland Field. Operational, for use by Manhattan

42-65321 42-65386 42-65385
42-65381 44-27285

4. One aircraft, 42-76259. Operational at Fort Worth Army Air Base.

5. Eighteen aircraft were in storage in the following depots and according to AMC records, had already been stripped of Silverplate equipment. These were the initial aircraft delivered to the 509th Composite Group and lacked the more advanced modifications being used by 1946, such as fuel injection, solar collection rings, Winkler type bomb-bay door and bomb-bay heating.

a. Seven at Davis-Monthan, Arizona

42-65209 42-65238 42-65235 42-65264 42-65237 42-65239
42-56260

b. Seven at Pyote, Texas

42-65216 42-65210 42-65236 42-65258 42-65259 42-65261
42-65263

c. One, 42-65217, at Victorville, California

d. One, 42-65262, at Warner-Robbins Air Materiel Command Depot.

e. Two at Davis-Monthan Field, Arizona, for delivery to the Army Air Forces Museum. 41-27297 “Bock’s Car” 44-86292 “Enola Gay”

6. Four aircraft had been salvaged and AMC records indicated Silverplate modifications had been removed, prior to reclamation.
42-65287 at Kirtland Field, as of 12th March 1946
44-27296 at Roswell Field 9th April. 1946
41-27303 washed out at Chicago, with reclamation complete, 31st October 1945.
44-86173 at Roswell. Reclamation completed 9th April 1946.

7. Nineteen new B-29s were being modified on Project DOX515. Sixteen serial numbers had already been chosen and the others were to be supplied within a short time (1947).
45-21736 44-86444 45-21739 44-86445 44-86401 44-86447 44-86437
44-86448 44-86439 44-86451 44-86440 44-87752 44-86443 44-87771
45-21818 44-87774

Silverplate Boeing B-29 Superfortress, 44-86292, “Enola Gay”

Appendix 9

Avro Lancaster Nuclear Bomber

7.81 *The first activities of the delivery program began in June 1943, when N. F. Ramsey (then still working with the Air Force) undertook to investigate available planes, with respect to their bomb carrying capacity. The only plane which would fit this requirement was the B-29, which, even so, could carry the bomb only by joining the bomb bays. The possibility of wing-carriage by other planes had been considered and rejected. At this time, it appeared that there might be considerable difficulty in obtaining a test B-29. Another plane, capable of carrying the bomb was the British Lancaster and some investigation was made of the possibility of using this plane. In terms of standardization of maintenance, however, this plane would have been difficult to operate from American bases. It was therefore decided that the B-29 would have to be used. SOURCE:-Manhattan District History: Book VIII, Volume 2, Project "Y" History, Technical, Doctor David Hawkins, Revision date 29th April 1947. VII-36, Page 216.* (If the device was to have been used in Europe, the Lancaster would have delivered it.)

Superfortress and Lancaster VIIs in formation

Appendix 10

Alexander Lippisch

Helmuth Walter

Kennedy and MacMillan

Truman and Clem Attlee (seated R)

Quebec conference 1943

Eisenhower and MacMillan, June 1958

CANBERRA

VALIANT

VICTOR

VULCAN

British Nuclear Devices

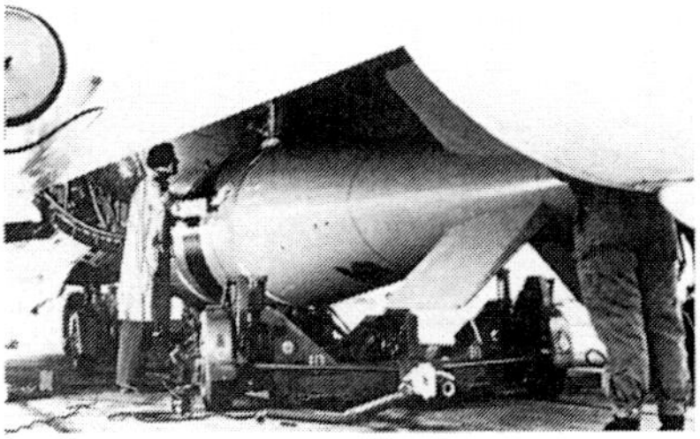

Valiant B.2

Valiant B.2, Pathfinder, low level nuclear bomber, cancelled and used for destructive trials. First flight 11th April 1952, acknowledged as being many years ahead of the specification.

RAF Aircraft
Part of the V Bomber timescale

DHC-1 Chipmunk, primary trainer, 12 AEF, RAF Turnhouse

Percival Provost T1 two-seat trainer

Hastings T5, B.C.B.S./S.C.B.S. RAF Lindholme

Dominie Navigation Trainer

Vickers Varsity T1, crew trainer used at Lindholme, Topcliffe, etc.

De Havilland Vampire T11 jet trainer

United States Air Force Nuclear-Capable Aircraft

Boeing B-50

Convair B-36

F-100F

Lockheed F-104

Boeing B-47

Republic F-105

Douglas B-66

F-4 Phantom

Ядерные бомбардировщики СССР

All names N.A.T.O. reporting codes

TU-4 Bull, Soviet copy of the B-29

TU-95 Bear

Myasishchev M-4 Bison

TU-16 Badger

Myasishchev M-50 Bounder

IL-28 Beagle

Appendix 11

Quebec Agreement
August 19th 1943

The Citadel, Quebec.

Articles of Agreement Governing Collaboration between the Authorities of the U.S.A. and the U.K. in the Matter of Tube Alloys
Whereas it is vital to our common safety in the present War to bring the Tube Alloys project to fruition at the earliest moments; and
Whereas this maybe more speedily achieved if all available British and American brains and resources are pooled; and
Whereas owing to war conditions it would be an improvident use of war resources to duplicate plants on a large scale on both sides of the Atlantic and therefore a far greater expense has fallen upon the United States;
It is agreed between us

> *First, that we will never use this agency against each other.*
> *Secondly, that we will not use it against third parties without each other's consent.*
> *Thirdly, that we will not either of us communicate any information about Tube Alloys to third parties except by mutual consent.*
> *Fourthly, that in view of the heavy burden of production falling upon the United States as the result of a wise division of war effort, the British Government recognize that any post-war advantages of an industrial or commercial character shall be dealt with as between the United States and Great Britain on terms to be specified by the President of the United States to the Prime Minister of Great Britain. The Prime Minister expressly disclaims any interest in these industrial and commercial aspects beyond what may be considered by the President of the United States to be fair and just and in harmony with the economic welfare of the world.*

And Fifthly, that the following arrangements shall be made to ensure full and effective collaboration between the two countries in bringing the project to fruition:
(a) There shall be set up in Washington a Combined Policy Committee composed of:

> *The Secretary of War. (United States), Dr. Vannevar Bush. (United States) Dr. James B. Conant. (United States), Field-Marshal Sir John Dill, G.C.B., C.M.G., D.S.O. (United Kingdom), Colonel the Right Hon. J. J.*

Llewellin, C.B.E., M.C., M.P. (United Kingdom), The Honourable C. D. Howe. (Canada)
The functions of this Committee, subject to the control of the respective Governments, will be:
(1) To agree from time to time upon the programme of work to be carried out in the two countries.
(2) To keep all sections of the project under constant review.
(3) To allocate materials, apparatus and plant, in limited supply, in accordance with the requirements of the programme agreed by the Committee.
(4) To settle any questions which may arise on the interpretation or application of this Agreement.

(b) There shall be complete interchange of information and ideas on all sections of the project between members of the Policy Committee and their immediate technical advisers.

(c) In the field of scientific research and development there shall be full and effective interchange of information and ideas between those in the two countries engaged in the same sections of the field.

(d) In the field of design, construction and operation of large-scale plants, interchange of information and ideas shall be regulated by such ad hoc arrangements as may, in each section of the field, appear to be necessary or desirable if the project is to be brought to fruition at the earliest moment. Such ad hoc arrangements shall be subject to the approval of the Policy Committee.
Aug. 19th 1943

Approved
Franklin D. Roosevelt
Winston S. Churchill

Condensed Bibliography

Periodicals and Books

Air Clues, Joint Services Recognition Journal, Royal Air Force Flying Review, Flying Review International, Air Enthusiast, Air International, Aeroplane, Journal of the Royal Naval Scientific Service, Flight, Aeroplane Monthly, Air Pictorial, Glasgow Herald, The Bulletin, Aeroplane Spotter, Aeronautics, Meccano Magazine, Hansard, Royal Air Force Historical Society Journals and Proceedings, Aircraft Illustrated, Aircraft Illustrated Extra, Air Training Corps Gazette, Airfix Magazine, Illustrated London News, Engineer, Engineering, Sphere, Air Reserve Gazette, l'Aerophile, Journal of Strategic Studies, etc.

1. Nuclear Deterrent Forces, Humphry Wynn, HMSO1994
2. Operation Grapple, Kenneth Hubbard/ Michael Simmons, Ian Allan, 1985
3. Statements Relating to the Atomic Bomb, HMSO, 1945
4. Manhattan District History: Book I - General; Volume 4 - Auxiliary Activities; Chapter 8 - Press Releases; Part II, 1945
5. Manhattan District History; Book VIII - Los Alamos Project (Y); Volume 2 Technical, 1947
6. The British Mission, article, Los Alamos Science, Winter/Spring Denis C. Fakley, 1983
7. Britain and Atomic Energy, 1939-1945, Margaret Gowing, HMSO1982
8. Avro Aircraft since 1908, A.J. Jackson, 1965.
9. German Aircraft Industry, Bremen Hamburg Area, CIOS Item No 25, Aircraft, G2 SHAEF, June 18, 1945.
10. Administration of War Production, Scott & Hughes, HMSO 1955
11. German Research in WW2, Leslie Simon, 1947.
12. B.I.O.S. Technical Index of Reports on German Industry, Alphabetical Subject index to CIOS, BIOS, FIAT and JIOA reports, British Intelligence Objectives Sub-Committee, Board of Trade, G2, SHAEF, 1946
13. Aeronautical Research Committee (ARC), Reports and Memorandum, annual technical reports 1920 to 1945, HMSO London.
14. Aeronautical Research Council, Reports and Memorandum, annual technical reports 1945 to 1980, HMSO, London.
15. German Aircraft of the Second World War. Antony L. Kay, E.J. Creek, J.R. Smith, Putnam, London, 1972.
16. National Advisory Committee for Aeronautics, Reports 1917-1958, U.S. Government Printing Office, Washington D.C.
17. Science at War, J.G. Crowther, R. Whiddington, HMSO 1947
18. Shavings for Breakfast, the History of Morris Furniture, 1884-1975 C. Mac Kay, A. MacKay, Glasgow, 2013
19. Pilot's Notes, Vulcan, MoS, 1964
20. Missile and Space Launches through 1970, Mark C. Cleary, USAF., N.D.
21. Project MX 776, REPORT NO. 56-981-021-46, Bell Aircraft, 1956
22. Britain, Australia and the Bomb, Lorna Arnold and Mark Smith, MoD, 1987
23. Preliminary flight investigation of a model of the Bell MX776, NACA, 1951
24. British Nuclear Policy Making, C. J. Bowie, A. Platt, USAF, January, 1983
25. The Royal Navy and British Security Policy, J E Oldham, 1982
26. The Nassau Connection, (Polaris) Peter Nailor, HMSO, 1988
27. Ideas, Concepts, Doctrine: Basic Thinking in the United States Air Force

1961-1984 (Volume 2), 1989.
28. A.R.D.E. REPORT (s) 26/55 Investigation of Accidental Explosion of a 1000lb bomb Marham, D.E. Jarrett, 1955
29. Aircraft of the Royal Air Force since 1918, Owen Thetford, 1968.
30. Aircraft Profiles, 54, 66, 162 et al, Edit Charles W. Cain, 1966-74
31. B-29 Flight Manual Vol 1 et 2, 1945
32. BIOS, German Aircraft Industry, W. Swallow, K. Lucas, SHAEF/B.of T., 1945
33. Radar and Controlled Missiles, Paris Area, CIOS 1-1, Major N.D. Crane, SHAEF, 1945
34. A Brief History of Early Unmanned Aircraft, J.F. Keane / S.S.Carr, ND
35. Precision Guided Munitions: Constructing a Bomb More Potent than the A-Bomb, Paul G. Gillespie, Dissertation, 2002
36. German Technical Aid to Japan, volumes 1 - 5, Military Intelligence Service, G, 2 Sept 1945
37. The heat of combustion of Jumbo, W. Penney, Trinity, 1944 (Paper)
38. Nuclear Weapons of the United States, James N. Gibson, Schiffer, 1996
39. Pilot's Notes, Victor BMk2 Blue Steel MoS, 1964.
40. The Development of Strategic Air Command, J.T. Bohn, O.O.T.H., 1976
41. Pilot's Notes Valiant Mk1 Aircraft, MoS, 1958
42. The Development of the German Air Force, R. Suchenwirth, USAF, 1968
43. Operation Backfire, in Volumes, HMSO, 1946
44. Operation Hurricane, Prime Minister's reply, Hansard, ND
45. Jahrbuch der Lufthart, Werner von Langsdorff, Munchen, 1931
46. Jet, The Story of a Pioneer, Frank Whittle, Pan, 1953
47. The Development of German Anti-aircraft Weapons and Equipment of All Types up to 1945, von Renz, USAF, 1958
48. The Organization of the German Air Force High Command and Higher Echelon Headquarters within the German Air Force, Bruno Maass, USAF.1955
49. Technical Training within the German Luftwaffe, by Werner Kreipe and Rudolf Koester, edited by Karl Gundelach, USAF, 1955.
50 The Development of German Aircraft Armament to 1945, by Oberst-Ing. Mix, USAF, 1957.
51. Bomber, Len Deighton, 1970.
52. Air Force Project (English Copy), The Reichswehr and Soviet Russia, by Wilhelm Spiedel, SHAEF, Historical Division, 1949
53. NACA report 1170, REPORT ON ROCKET POWER PLANTS BASED ON T SUBSTANCE Helmuth Walter, (Translation), 1947
54. Command and Leadership in the German Air Force, Prof. Richard Suchenwirth, USAF, 1969.

55. Rocket Development, Liquid Fuel Rocket Research, 1929 – 1941, Robert H. Goddard, Esther C. Goddard (Edit.), 1948
56. British Nuclear Policymaking, Christopher J. Bowie, Alan Platt, USAF, 1984.
57. A.P.3365, Notes on the Royal Air Force, Air Ministry, 1962
58. Centenary Journal, 1866-1966, Royal Aeronautical Society, 1966
59. Seeing off the Bear, Proceedings of the Royal Air Force Historical Society, R G Miller (Ed.) USAF, 1995
60. Rolls-Royce and the Mustang, David Birch, Historical Series 9, Rolls-Royce Heritage Trust, 1987
61. Bomber Squadrons of the RAF and their Aircraft, P.B.J.R Moyes, Macdonald, 1964
62. The British Bomber since 1914, Francis K. Mason, Putnam, 1994
63. Beardmore Aviation, Charles E. Mac Kay, A. MacKay, 2012
64. The Fedden Mission to Germany, Final Report, M.A.P., C.I.O.S 104, 1945
66. Enemy Ordnance Material (German), O.C.O.O., U.S., June 1945
67. Encyclopaedia of U.S. Air Force Aircraft and Missile Systems, Vol II, Marcelle Size Knaack, O.O.A.F.H., 1975
68. The Rise and fall of the German Air force, Air Ministry, R.P. No248, 1948
69. Services textbook of explosives, Defence Council, M.O.D., Mar. 1972
70. Report number 43, Report on Hydrogen Peroxide, Part 2, MIT 1953
71. Arms Control and British and French Nuclear Forces, Mary J. Schroeder, Department of the Navy, 1987
72. The Royal Navy and British Security Policy, James Edmond Oldham, Department of the Navy, 1983
73. Missile Aerodynamics, AGARD 98, (ORGANISATION DU TRAITE DE L'ATLANTIQUE NORD), February 1979
74. The British Nuclear Deterrent, Nicholas K. J. Witney, Project Air Force, Rand, 1995
75. National Security Archive Electronic Briefing Book No. 159, NSA, 2005